Beat the Tea

By the same author

THE SECOND BOOK OF JIGSAW
PUZZLES
JIGSAW PUZZLES 4
PUZZLE TRAIL

Beat The Teacher

Clive Doig
Illustrated by Malcolm Bird

BBC/KNIGHT BOOKS.

Copyright © British Broadcasting Corporation 1985

Illustrations copyright © British Broadcasting Corporation 1985

First published 1985 by BBC/Knight Books

British Library C.I.P.

Doig, Clive
  Beat the teacher.
  1. Games———Juvenile literature
  I. Title   II. Bird, Malcolm
  790   GV1203

  ISBN 0 340 38088 8
       0 563 20428 1 (BBC)

This book is sold subject to the condition that it shall not, by way of trade or otherwise, be lent, re-sold, hired out or otherwise circulated without the publisher's prior consent in any form of binding or cover other than that in which it is published and without a similar condition including this condition being imposed on the subsequent purchaser.

Printed and bound in Great Britain for the British Broadcasting Corporation, 35 Marylebone High Street, London W1M 4AA and Hodder and Stoughton Paperbacks, a division of Hodder and Stoughton Ltd., Mill Road, Dunton Green, Sevenoaks, Kent (Editorial Office: 47 Bedford Square, London WC1B 3DP) by Cox & Wyman Ltd., Reading.

INTRODUCTION

Beat the Teacher first appeared on BBC 1 in September 1984 and was shown four days a week for seven weeks. The programme was devised to enable teachers and pupils to pit their wits fairly and equally against each other. Naturally teachers will usually have more knowledge in most subjects than children. So what subjects can be found for a competitive quiz between adults and thirteen-year-olds in which the advantage does not lie with the adult?

There are skills which do not depend on either acquired knowledge, memory or learning. Skills such as speed of reaction, intuition, observation, instant recall, for example. *Beat the Teacher* made use of questions which required these skills and added other factors – some luck, some silliness and a new game, which required tactics. So, given an impartial environment, would adults and children have an equal chance? Well, in the 1984 series there were twenty-eight contests between pupils and teachers. And in thirteen of these the winners were the children!

Of course speed and the choice of alternative answers allow the quick-thinking contestant to do well. Such ingredients as speed and performers' nerves – the glare of the television lights, the clamour of the audience, the tension imposed by the cameras – cannot be reproduced in a book. However, if you want to set up your own 'Beat the Teacher' contest (or better still a 'Beat the Parent' contest), using the book, follow the rules of the game on page 7. If you are alone, just see how many questions you can answer. Try and answer as fast as possible. A maximum of 5 minutes per page should enable you to study the alternatives and work out the answers. When you do the 'Observation' questions, study the pictures for 30 seconds and then see how many of the questions you can answer before turning back to check. Occasionally there are pages of really silly trick questions. With these the time limit should be one minute and you should not have to look up the answers. Once you have mastered all these you should be able to beat anybody!

The winners of the first series of *Beat the Teacher* were the pupils and teachers of Monk's Walk School, Welwyn Garden City, Hertfordshire.

In 1985 another knock-out competition between schools has been arranged, followed by an 'Individual Champions' run, where either a single boy or girl, or a teacher, another adult or even a celebrity will run as champion until defeated. Next year, it could be you! By reading this book and trying out the questions you too could *Beat the Teacher*

BEAT THE TEACHER

THE GAME

The Board

Ordinary Noughts and Crosses or Tick-Tack-Toe is a well-known and pretty easy game to play, but that is not necessarily so on *Beat The Teacher*.

Although the principle, to get a row of 0's or X's, is the same, it is a matter of answering the questions correctly before another contestant does so, and then turning one or more of the nine squares in the grid to the right symbol.

Each square in the grid on the Noughts and Crosses board turns and is capable of showing either 0 or X or a Blank. The board pictured above is showing 9 Blanks, as it does at the beginning of each contest.

Each square turns in a standard order, which is: Blank–0–Blank–X, but as all Blanks look the same you do not know whether an 0 or an X will come up next. For instance, turning each of the squares once on the blank board above could result in the board as shown below:

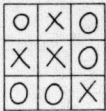

Four X's and Five 0's

But of course you now know the sequence of each square, because if you were to move the bottom-right square twice it would in sequence go Blank–0, and two lines of three 0's would be completed. If you moved each of the squares one turn, then the board would be full of blanks again, and if you

5

moved each of them four times it would look the same as it is now. The tactics of the game are quite far-reaching once you have mastered the rules.

The Rules

One contestant plays Noughts, the other Crosses. Each correct answer is awarded with a certain number of moves on the grid. The first contestant to answer correctly is awarded moves as follows:

A Quickie or Trick question . . . 1 move
A question with two or three alternative answers [a), b) or a) b) c)] . . . 2 moves
A question with four alternative answers [a) b) c) or d)] . . . 3 moves
A question without alternatives . . . 4 moves

The successful contestant must then use all of these moves to turn one or more of the squares on the grid to their best advantage. For example, if awarded three moves, these three moves can be used to turn one square three times; or to move two squares, one twice and one once, or to move three squares once each.

At the beginning of a game the board shows blanks, but the squares have been randomly set so that nobody knows whether a 0 or an X will turn up next.

The object of turning the squares round is to try to make a row or rows of three of the contestant's own symbol. Doing so accrues points as set out below:

Scoring

Three symbols in a row . . . 5 points.
More than one row, across, up, down or diagonally, on the same go . . . 5 points per row.
Here are some examples from diagram A:

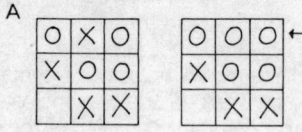

Moving the top-centre square from X to 0 would give the person playing Noughts, 5 points. Whereas moving the bottom-right square from X to 0 would give Noughts 10 points – 5 for the row on the right and 5 for the diagonal row.

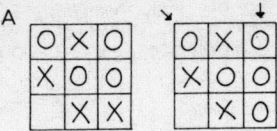

If a contestant fills the whole board with his or her symbol he and she is awarded an extra 20 points and the board is returned to the start, all blanks.

There is a time limit of ten seconds for answering questions, and the same limit for deciding how to use your moves.

The game is over after twelve minutes of play, and the winner is the contestant with the highest number of points scored on the Noughts and Crosses board.

The Joker

Each contestant is also allotted a joker, which can be played at any time during the game, before a question has been started. The advantage of the joker is that it completely reverses all the symbols on the board; i.e.: all 0's become X's and all X's become 0's. The person who has played the joker will be awarded the points for all rows of his or her symbol now on the board, if the next question is answered correctly.

For example, if the board looks like diagram B and Crosses plays his joker.

B

		X
0	0	
0	X	0

The board is then immediately changed to:

X		0
X	X	
X	0	X

Crosses will be awarded the 10 points for the two rows of X's if he can answer the next question correctly, if not, the board remains the same but he scores nothing. The person playing Noughts may not now use the joker for another three minutes of play. (This is to stop the immediate use of the other joker to reverse the positions again.)

The contestants can only use their jokers once.

Sample Game

Here is an example of an actual game:

The contestant playing Noughts was a girl pupil, the contestant playing Crosses was a man teacher.

The board at the start.

Question 1: Noughts correct: 4 moves. She uses one move in each of the corners.

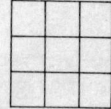

Noughts was lucky on 2 squares and unlucky on 2.
No score

Question 2: Crosses correct: 3 moves. He uses two moves top-right, one move top-centre.

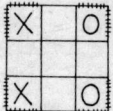

Crosses scores 5 points. (*Score* Crosses 5 – Nought 0)

8

Question 3: Crosses correct: 1 move. He uses it on left-centre.

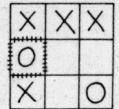

Unluckily it is a 0.
Score Crosses 5 – Noughts 0.

Question 4: Crosses correct: 2 moves. He uses both on left-centre.

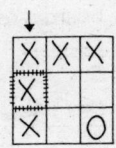

Crosses knows that 2 moves will give him another row.
Crosses scores 5 points.
Score Crosses 10 – Noughts 0.

Question 5: Noughts correct: 3 moves. She uses one move top-left, one top-right and one bottom-left.

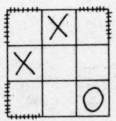

This tactic means that in each of these corners Crosses will have to turn the squares 3 times to get back to his symbol.
Score Crosses 10 – Noughts 0.

Question 6: Crosses correct: 3 moves. He uses one move on central square, one bottom-centre, one right-centre.

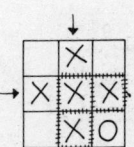

Crosses is very lucky again getting first time X's in these squares.
Crosses scores 10 points for 2 rows.
Score Crosses 20 – Noughts 0.

Question 7: Noughts
correct: 2 moves. She
uses both on the
bottom-right.

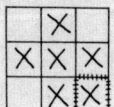

Noughts strangely gives
her opponent an 'X'. No
score, but good tactics:
why?
No score.

Noughts plays her joker. The board is reversed:

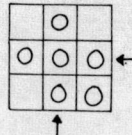

There are 10 points for Noughts if she gets the next question correct.

Question 8: Noughts correct. Noughts scores 10 points.

Question 9: Crosses
correct: 2 moves. He
uses them to move the
central square twice.

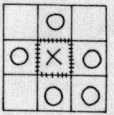

Score Crosses
20 – Noughts 10.

Question 10: Noughts
correct: 1 move. She
moves top-right.

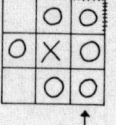

Noughts scores 5 points.
Score Crosses
20 – Noughts 15.

Question 11: Crosses correct: 3 moves. He uses them twice on bottom-right, once for top-left.

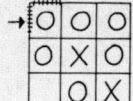

A terrible blunder by Crosses in the top-left square, giving points to Noughts. Noughts scores 5 points.
Score Crosses 20 – Noughts 20.

Question 12: Noughts correct: 4 moves. She uses two on the central square, two bottom-right.

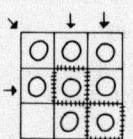

Noughts scores 20 points.
Score Crosses 20 – Noughts 40.
(NB: Crosses cannot play his joker yet.)

Question 13: Crosses correct: 1 move. He uses it on the central square.

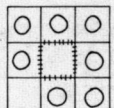

No score.

Question 14: Noughts correct: 2 moves. She uses one bottom-left, one on the central square.

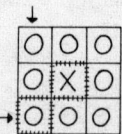

Noughts scores 10 points.
Score Crosses 20 – Noughts 50.

Crosses plays his joker. The board is reversed:

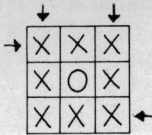

Question 15: Crosses correct so he picks up the 20 points available.

Score Crosses 40 – Noughts 50.

Question 16: Noughts correct: 2 moves. She uses one top-right, one bottom-left.

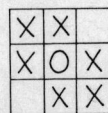

No score.

END OF GAME FINAL SCORE Noughts 50 – Crosses 40.

Noughts, the girl pupil, beat Crosses, the man teacher. She 'Beat The Teacher'.

But only just, because if Crosses had answered the last question correctly he would have had a complete board of X's and 20 more points.

As can be seen from this example, the playing of the joker can be crucial, and it is always best to try and wait until the last possible moment to play it.

If you just want to see how well you would do on the programme against your teacher, then just give yourself points instead of moves as you answer the questions in the book. Play against your mum or dad and get the other to read out the questions. After 20 questions tot up your scores. If you can beat your parents you should have a good chance of beating a teacher.

1. Alan has three times as many marbles as John, who has twice as many as Barbara, who has one. How many must Alan give away so they all have the same number?
a) 2 b) 3 c) 4 d) Can't be done

2.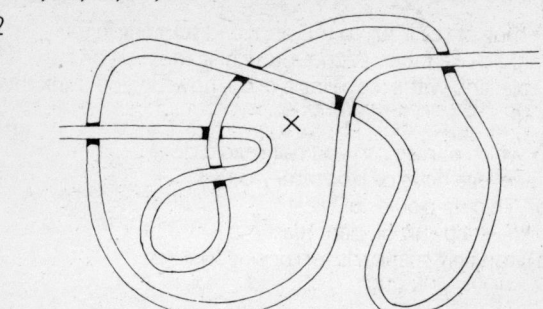

If you pull both ends of the rope, will it trap the post at X?
a) Yes b) No

3. Two boys have girl friends. One is in a tissue factory, the other in Unilever. Who are they?
a) Tessa and Una b) Nell and Sue c) Len and Sis d) Eve and Sue

4. Alf was imprisoned, naked, in a sound-proof room in Aberystwyth. The walls, ceiling and floors of the room were padded, without any windows or visible doors. But he still got a message to a friend in Brighton. How?

5. Four horses in a race. Bright Star came two places behind All at Sea. Give us a Kiss was in the first three, and Pottipop wasn't. Who won?

6. Small people like tall people, so what do smelly people like?
a) Clean people b) Ugly people c) Telly people d) Wizards

7. If 1981 is to 1861, what is 1068 to?
a) 8901 b) 1908 c) 8091 d) 8601

8. A three-letter word has been replaced in this story, what is it? 'A couple of spottily dressed pot-pot dancers from Potnes, potoed down a potyon in Potada, and saw a toupot eating a potato. If a toupot pot do it, pot you?'
a) tar b) car c) can d) man

13

9   Nine numbers are to be seen in this sentence, but somehow three of them are written out backwards. Which one of these backwards numbers is even?
    a)Two b)Six c)Nine d)Ten

10 A mug of tea is full to the brim and standing in the middle of a table. Without touching the mug or the table, and without spilling a drop, how do you drink the lot?

11 In which phrase can you not read a dog?
    a)College boys oil laboratory doors
    b)Whip up oodles of cream
    c)Have a picnic or giant feast
    d)Stop ugly spaniards terrorising tourists

12

Two buckets on the left are full of precious liquid. How many pourings, using the container on the right, do you need to measure out exactly 4 litres of liquid, without throwing away a drop?
a)1 b)6 c)4 d)Can't be done

13 If you had a pair of oranges, a pair of apples and a pear, and pared them in half, how many halves of fruit would you have?
    a)10 b)5 c)6 d)16

14 What is the next in this sequence: Jan, Jun, Nov, Apr?
    a)Sep b)Jul c)Dec d)Feb

15 If Sunday, Monday and Friday have something in common, what is in common with Thursday?
    a)Tuesday b)Saturday c)Wednesday

16 A typewriter makes an error with one letter. If it types out 'Egglagd', what would it type for its capital?
    a)Logdong b)Eggnog c)Loggod d)Logdog

14

17 A tiger lay on the ground directly between a boy and his hut. It was broad daylight and the boy had no weapon, but he managed to walk right over the tiger straight to his hut without being harmed. How?

18 A patch of grass 5 metres square has a goat tethered on a 3½-metre rope at each corner. Will any grass escape their grazing?
a) Yes b) No c) Depends on how hungry they are d) Depends on how far they go

19 If [figure] is to [figure]

What is [figure] to ?

a) [figure] b) [figure] c) [figure] d) [figure]

20 Which of these anagraminals does not come from Australia?
a) Goronaka b) Blaylaw c) Bamtow d) Growhat

21 If you have six 10p coins and three 1p coins, can you pay for an article costing 10p exactly?
a) Yes b) No

22 Alternately two of us take sweets from a bag containing an odd number. You start. If I give you my last sweet, how many more have you had than me?
a) 0 b) 1 c) 2 d) 3

23 There are four black and four white pebbles in a bag, Johnny takes three which are white, Ted takes two black and one white. What are the chances that Mary will take three pebbles of the same colour?
a) 50% b) No chance c) Certain

24 LUIGI, ANNIE and PAULA all have something in common with one of these names, which?
a)LOUIS b)CLARE c)PETER d)BERYL

25 The sign is pointing the opposite direction to what it says. Which way is the man facing?
a)South b)West c)East

26 If you had one apple, two potatoes, three swedes and four oranges, how many fruit would you have?
a)10 b)5 c)8 d)1

27 If Spurs beat QPR 3–1 in the first leg of the Milk Cup, and QPR beat Spurs 4–3 in the return match, who won on aggregate?
a)Spurs b)QPR c)It was a draw

28 You play one side of a music cassette, stop after ⅔ of the side, then turn it over. How much of the tape must you rewind to get to the start of the second side?
a)⅓ b)⅔ c)You can't

29
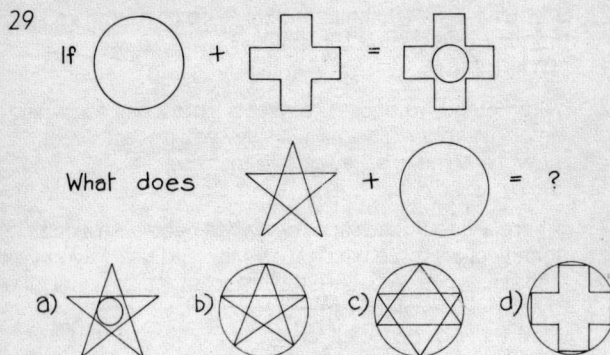

30. How many openings has a jumper?
    a)3 b)4 c)2 d)None

31. In the singing of 'Auld Lang Syne' it is customary to cross over your arms and link hands with the person next to you. Which hand of the person on your right are you holding?
    a)Left b)Right

32. If Jack is to Corner, what is Miss to?
    a)Magdalene b)Muffet c)Tuffet d)Spider

33. If you have a gallon of tea and a pint of milk, how many complete half-pint mugs of tea with milk can you make?
    a)None b)As many as you like c)16 d)18

34. Who invented the ball-point pen?
    a)Johnny Ball b)Georg and Laszlo Biró c)Queen Victoria d)Penelope Point

35. What can you see with your eyes shut?
    a)Nothing b)The stars c)Dreams d)The inside of your eyelids

QUICKIES

Try these rather tricky silly ones out on your friends!

36. Who sings the 'Star-Spangled Banner'?
    a)Australians b)Frogs c)Singers

37. What was Siam called before it was called Thailand?
    a)Indo-China b)Mapituraram c)Siam d)Honolulu

38. Who did the slayer of David slay?
    a)Goliath b)Sling and shot c)Fred d)David

39. What is the highest point of Ben Nevis?
    a)Ben Macduish b)The North slope c)The top

40. What nuts do you get from hazel trees?
    a)Walnuts b)Peanuts c)Hazelnuts d)Cobs

41. In which direction does the Amazon flow?
    a)Towards the centre b)To the Pacific c)Downstream d)Upstream

42. Short-sighted people have difficulty seeing?
    a)Small things b)Tall things c)Things far away d)Things too close

43   What is a lady mayor called?
    a)Mayor b)Mayoress c)The Missus

44   What colour is very similar to pink?
    a)Blue b)Green c)Lemon d)Rose

45   What does a palmist study?
    a)Palm trees b)Psalms c)Stars d)Hands

---

46   What is the weight of tuppenny rice and treacle in ounces?
    a)2 b)16 c)8 d)5

47   In Italy, traffic drives on the right. Which way do Italians drive round roundabouts?
    a)Clockwise b)Counter-clockwise c)Straight across d)Backwards

48   Still in Italy, you are riding a bicycle and want to turn left, on which side should you pull the handlebars towards you?
    a)Left b)Right c)In the middle

49   This is a picture of a dovetail joint, between two pieces of wood:

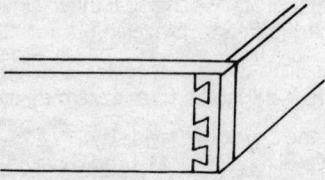

    What is wrong with it?

50   A mole has to eat its weight in worms every day of its life. But in any one field there is only a hundred times the weight of worms for each mole. How does each mole survive more than a hundred days?
    a)It doesn't b)It eats figs instead c)The worms reproduce d)The mole diets

51   Six birds sit on a roof. You make a noise to scare them off, and all but four of them fly away, how many are left?
    a)2 b)4 c)0

52 You have some bookshelves, 15cm deep, the length of your room; but there is only 25cm between each shelf. What is the easiest method of putting books which are 50cm high on to the shelves?
a)Cut each book in half b)Unscrew the shelves and reposition them c)Cut out slots in the shelf above d)Lay them down flat

53 What tree does a conker come from?
a)Conifer b)Sweet chestnut c)Horse chestnut d)Spanish chestnut

54 What could 'HIJKLMNO' stand for?
a)Water b)Napoleon c)Hijack Lemons! d)Liverpool

55 It is approximately 70 miles between each degree of longitude at the equator, how far is it between each degree of longitude at the South Pole?
a)70 miles b)35 miles c)11 inches d)Nothing

56 If you kneel on the floor with your hands on your hips, which of these parts of your body is furthest away from the ceiling?
a)Elbows b)Knees c)Hands d)Heels

57 Two letters on a typewriter have only produced splodges on this letter you receive from a friend: *HI* *E**LEMEN* I* *URROUNDED BY *HI**LE*, PLEA*E *END *OME KILLER. What should you take with you?
a)Guns b)Michael Jackson LP c)Moth-balls d)Weed-killer

58 The words 'facetious' and 'abstemious' are similar in a certain way; what word below would be similar to 'unoriental' in the same way?
a)Obstreperous b)Unnoticeable c)Muscovite d)Subcontinental

59 What is the next letter in this sequence?
A B D O P ?
a)T b)U c)R d)Q

OBSERVATION ONE... THE FAMILY

Look at the picture opposite for exactly thirty seconds, time yourself, and then turn over the page and see how many of the questions about the picture you can answer without looking back.

OBSERVATION ONE ... THE FAMILY

How well have you remembered the picture overleaf? Try not to turn back and peek.

60 How many earrings is Tina, the eldest girl, wearing?
    a)0 b)1 c)2

61 How many gulls are there?
    a)8 b)3 c)5

62 What is Teddy, the smallest child, holding?
    a)A teddy b)Another person's hand c)A dummy

63 What is on Tony's shirt badge?
    a)Cross b)Castle c)Dog d)3 Fishes

64 How many shoes are there in the picture?
    a)9 b)8 c)5 d)4

65 Who is beneath the cloud?
    a)Tina b)Tessa c)Tom

66 What is on the horizon behind Tessa?
    a)House b)Tree c)Factory d)Train

67 How many persons have their arms folded?
    a)1 b)2 c)3

68 What is the artist's mistake?
    a)Tony not standing on ground b)Smoke going wrong way c)Horizon line missing d)Arm missing

69 Who is on the right of the picture?
    a)Teddy b)Tony c)Tessa d)Therese

---

70 How many centimetres are there in a hundredth of a metre?
    a)100 b)10 c)1 d)0

71 You receive the following note delivered by a messenger called Joe: 'The person delivering this note has read it and torn it up, and written another one in its place. So do not let on that you know the secret meeting is at 6 o'clock at Sam's place. Signed Bob.' Who wrote the note?
    a)Bob b)Sam c)Joe d)You can't tell

72 When is the meeting taking place?
a) 6 o'clock b) Now c) There is no meeting d) You can't tell

73 What is wrong with the note?
a) It should be in Swahili b) It wouldn't exist if it was torn up c) If it has been rewritten, Joe wouldn't have brought it d) Sam's trousers have fallen down

74 Who did Joe deliver the message to?

75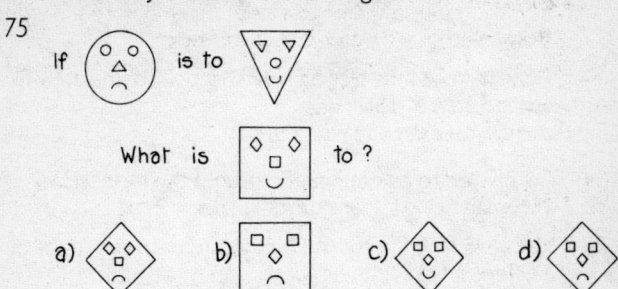

76 You receive another message, this time the letters M, N, R, T and W have been substituted for others: 'BEEF BE AF FEZ FO FEZ A.B. FOBOTTOM.' If it is midnight when you receive it, how long have you got?
a) ½ mile b) 10 hours 10 minutes c) 9 hours 50 minutes d) 1 day

77 Here is a top, side and end view of a well-known object, what is it?

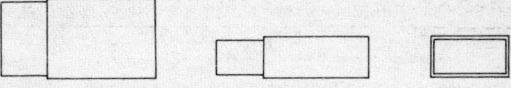

a) Book b) Door c) Television d) Matchbox

78 One of the statements below is false, which?
a) The third statement is written backwards
b) Sdrawkcab nettirw si tnemetats siht
c) Eslaf si tnemetats dnoces eht
d) The first statement is true

79 If a man and a woman have two children and each child has two children, and each grandchild has two children, what is the total of the man and woman's offspring?
a) 14 b) 16 c) 8 d) 12

80 If 36 is to 27, and 19 is to 83, what is 51 to ?
    a)32 b)79 c)112 d)201

81 What do peaches, nectarines, avocados and plums have that lemons do not?
    a)Eatable flesh b)Juice c)Skin d)A stone

82 A coin is engraved with the date 54BC, when was it made?
    a)54BC b)During Julius Caesar's reign c)Before the Roman Empire d)After Christ was born

83 How many whole tiles 5cm × 10cm will completely fill a space 15cm × 15cm?
    a)4 b)5 c)12 d)They won't

84 Compared to its size, what can jump the furthest?
    a)Human being b)Hare c)Human flea d)Frog

85 Mr Black, Miss Spotty and Mrs White each own a car of a different type to their name

    If Miss Spotty is immediately behind the car in front, what type is Mrs White's car?
    a)Spotty b)Black c)Blue d)There is not enough information to know

86 A school notice, with two letters missing, read: 'A wel was slen from the ilet night. Would the simplen who ok it, please return it Mr. Ily in the sres morrow.' What are the two letters together?
    a)ly b)vo c)to d)we

87 Which of the following inventions came first?
    a)Radio b)Telephone c)Television d)Electricity

88 What is the next in this sequence?
    E 2 G 6 G 5 E 7 ?
    a)G b)V c)F

89 What is the furthest the average human eye can see?
    a)50 miles b)250,000 miles c)Over 90 million miles d)13.53 miles

90. Which of these birds swims the fastest?
a) Duck b) Drake c) Penguin d) Sparrow

91. Which is the shortest piece of string?

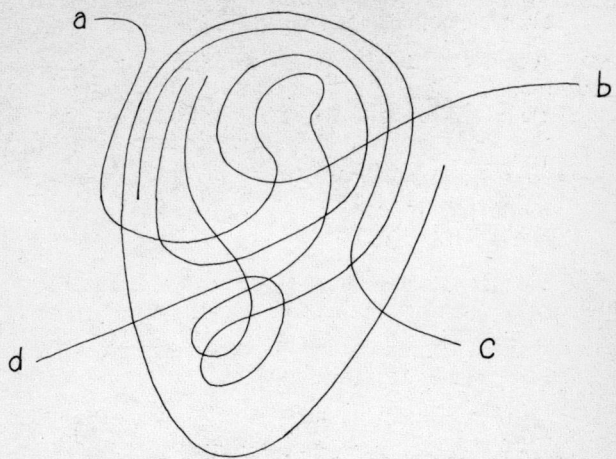

92. When was Queen Elizabeth first called Queen Elizabeth the First?
a) 1558 b) When she was crowned c) When Queen Elizabeth II became Queen d) Friday 15 March 1605

93. Which of these letters could never occur doubly in an English word?
a) i b) z c) q d) a

94. Which city is furthest east?
a) Hong Kong b) London c) It depends where you are d) Rome e) New York

95. Which city is furthest east of London?
a) Bristol b) Paris c) Tokyo d) Los Angeles

96. Which of the following was not invented by humans?
a) Nylon b) Rayon c) Silk d) Plastic

97. What have peanuts, potatoes, beetroot and swedes in common?
a) You can't eat them raw b) They all came originally from Peru c) They grow under the ground d) They are all ingredients of Christmas cake

OBSERVATION TWO ... THE SEASIDE

Another observation test. Look at this picture for thirty seconds and then turn over the page and answer the questions.

OBSERVATION TWO... THE SEASIDE

What have you remembered from the picture?

98 What is the mermaid sitting on?
    a)The pier b)Deckchair c)A rock d)A breakwater

99 What is the mermaid saying?
    a)'Woof!' b)'Hi!' c)'Shark!' d)'Sh!'

100 What has mother been reading?
    a)Book b)Newspaper c)Letter

101 How many buckets are there?
    a)1 b)2 c)3 d)0

102 What has been left out of the picnic hamper?
    a)Fork b)Plate c)Cup d)Sandwich

103 What is father about to meet?
    a)K9 b)A dog c)The mermaid d)A shark

104 Which way is the steamship travelling?
    a)Left b)Right

105 What is on top of the picnic hamper?
    a)Sunglasses b)Shoe c)Watch d)Book

106 Which of mother's feet is the crab nearest?
    a)Left b)Right c)Same distance from both

107 What is on the flag on the sandcastle?
    a)2 bars b)2 dots c)2 squares d)cross

---

108 The tall man said the small man said that the tall man said a rude word. The fat man said the small man was lying. Did the tall man say a rude word?
    a)Yes b)No c)Not enough information

109 In which country can you find a girl?
    a)Zimbabwe b)Bulgaria c)Malawi d)Switzerland

110 What is the minimum number of times that the minute-hand of a clock passes over or under the hour-hand in any period of sixty minutes?
    a)Once b)Twice c)None

111 What part of your body, apart from your hair, keeps growing all your life?
    a)Nose b)Teeth c)Heart d)Nails

112 Here is a sad tale: 'Poor impoverished orphan boy, Jimmy Snuffit, died on his twentieth birthday, on 21 June, just before his mother told him he had won a million pounds on the pools.' What is wrong?

113 What is the opposite of 'Not in'?
a) Out b) Not Out

114 Which is the odd one out?

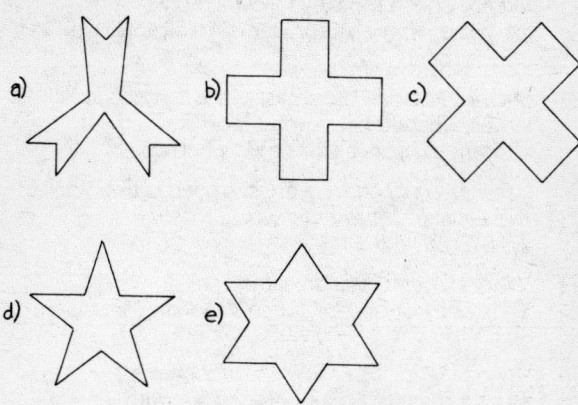

MORE QUICKIES

Try these tricky ones out on your friends!

115 On what river is Newcastle-upon-Tyne situated?
a) Tyne b) Wear c) Tees d) Thames

116 What do people on the uninhabited outer islands of Tonga speak?
a) Tongan b) Swedish c) Gabrimalli d) Nothing

117 When a candle is held upside-down, which way does the flame burn?
a) Up b) Down c) It doesn't

118 Who did Nelson say 'Kiss me Hardy' to?
a)His mother b)Hardy c)Jack Quick

119 The word 'igloo' is a loan word in English from the Eskimo language. What do the Eskimos call it?
a)Kwatakuitlak b)Ice House c)Igloo d)Glob

120 What was the furthest planet from the sun in our solar system before Pluto was discovered?
a)Neptune b)Io c)Pluto d)Venus

121 Where does a monkey follow a monk?
a)In a monastery b)Gibraltar c)In a dictionary d)On the underground

122 Stick insects look like sticks, and leaf insects look like leaves, what do tiger-moths look like?
a)Moths b)Tigers c)Lions d)Raspberries

123 If the letters Q and T were swapped in the order of the alphabet, what letter would follow R?
a)S b)Q c)U d)P

124 Who is Victoria Station named after?
a)Victoria Principal b)Queen Victoria c)Mr Station

125 If I am lying, and tell you that the poison in one of two glasses is not in the glass on the left, which one should you drink?
a)Left b)Right

126

If SHARK is to ƧHAᴙK

What is COD to?

a) ꓛOD b) DOC c) PLAICE d) COD

127 The new scoring system of the English Football League is three points for a win, one point for a draw. Is it possible for a side having played five games to have scored 13 points?
a)Yes b)No

128 What is the most common letter in this stupid sentence?
a)E b)T c)I

129 If you fold a square piece of paper exactly in half three times, what shape of paper do you get?
a)Square b)Diamond c)Triangle

130 You intercept the following coded message: 'Would one of Lenny's wives organise rendezvous Thursday, High Street.' Where is the meeting taking place?
a)The clock tower b)Leamington Station c)Woolworths

131 You have three pairs of different coloured socks in a drawer. How many single socks do you take out, without looking, to make certain that you have a matching pair?
a)4 b)3 c)2

132 You have a half-full cup of coffee, and a half-full cup of milk. Put a teaspoon of milk into the coffee and mix. Put a teaspoon of this mixture back into the milk. Have you now got:
a)More coffee in the milk than milk in the coffee
b)More milk in the coffee than coffee in the milk c)The same amount in both

133 Which backwards is spelt backwards?
a)SDRAKCAB b)SDRAWCKAB c)SDRAWKCAB d)BACKWARDS

134 In a code the letters 'LAD' are swapped with the letters 'BER' in that order. Which of the following would read BLADDER?
a)DREBBAL b)LBEDDAR c)LDERRAB d)LBERRAD

135 Which is the odd one out?
a)SPOT b)OPTS c)SOFT d)STOP

136 What word is from this sentence?
a)Seven b)that c)left d)missing

137 A flower, a fruit and a colour, which of the following names does not fit?
a)Olive b)Rose c)Viola d)Violet

31

138

How many complete circles are drawn here?
a) 8 b) 6 c) 5 d) 3

OBSERVATION THREE ... THE STREET

Look carefully at the picture opposite for thirty seconds, counting things and noticing everything you can, then turn over the page and answer the questions.

OBSERVATION THREE ... THE STREET

Try not to look back.

139 Which way is the bicycle pointing?
a)Left b)Right

140 What type of business does the shop on the right of the scene undertake?
a)Undertaker's b)Baker's c)Tailor's d)Butcher's

141 How many birds are sitting on the roof?
a)7 b)8 c)6

142 What is the furniture dealer's name?
a)Rogers b)Cambridge c)Dorx d)Kavatjian

143 What letter is missing from Len's Provisions shop?
a)L b)I c)V d)E

144 What is seen in the right-hand window above Rentabox?
a)Cat b)Vase of flowers c)Lampshade d)Candlestick

145 What else is on the pavement beside the nurse and pram?
a)Television set b)Dog c)Parking meter

146 How many chimney-pots are there?
a)8 b)10 c)6 d)4

147 As you look at Len's Provisions, which side is the door to the shop?
a)Left b)Centre c)Right

148 What number is the Undertaker's?
a)29 b)35 c)37 d)34

---

149 If you dial 9 on a telephone dial, what number shows through the first hole?
a)3 b)Nothing c)2 d)1

150 How many letters are there in the alphabet?
a)25 b)11 c)20 d)1

151 A combination lock has four wheels, each with the six numbers 0–5 on them. Starting at 0000, how many clicks round of the wheels will reach the number 2323?
a)10 b)9 c)8 d)12

152 What part of your body can you not touch with your left hand?
a) Left armpit b) Left knee c) Left elbow d) Small of your back

153 What word means: a sliver of wood, a piece of silicon, to chisel at, and a fried potato?
a) Bit b) Chip c) Crisp d) Splinter

154 If you take half of A/W− and double it what do you get?
a) 4 b) 5 c) 6 d) 7

8

155 How much carpet 4 metres wide do you need to cover the floor of this room?

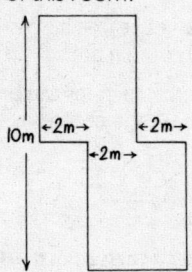

a) 20 metres b) 15 metres c) 10 metres

156 What is wrong with the stamp below?
a) Too many perforations b) Abbreviation for peseta is P c) 20 pesetas is too much d) It would say 'España' not Spain

157 You are standing in the Kalahari Desert in May. The average number of days it rains in May is only one. If it is sunny at noon on the 28th, what are the chances it will still be sunny 36 hours later?

158 If I call 'heads − tails' and 'tails − heads', and I tell you a coin is not heads up, what face is facing down?
a) Heads b) Tails

159 Brothers and sisters have I none,
    But this man's father is my father's son.
    Who am I looking at?
    a)My father b)Myself c)My son

160 If Sally likes jelly, William likes blackberry, and Annette
    likes beetroot, what does Jennifer like?
    a)Blackberry b)Apple c)Cheese d)Cinnamon

161 In where can you find a cat?
    a)cabin b)train c)watch d)truck

162 All ants climb at a rate of 30 feet a minute. How long
    would it take three ants to climb 10 feet?
    a)1 minute b)20 seconds c)3 minutes

163 In Camden market I came across a foreigner, what
    country did he come from?

164 Two 10p and two 1p coins can be laid down in a row
    symmetrical about the centre, as shown below:

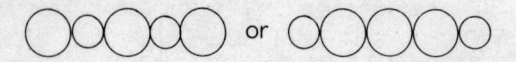

    ⚪⚪⚪⚪⚪ or ⚪⚪⚪⚪⚪

    If you had three of each coin, how many different
    symmetrical rows, about the centre, could you make?
    a)3 b)4 c)6 d)0

165 Three sisters married three brothers with the same
    names as theirs, but nobody married their own
    namesakes. If Pat had Bobby as a husband, who had Jo
    as a wife?
    a)Pat b)Joe c)Bobby d)Desmond

166 If the words 'yesterday' and 'tomorrow' had their
    meanings swapped round, what would the day after
    tomorrow week be if yesterday was Tuesday?
    a)Tuesday b)Monday c)Wednesday d)August

167 What is wrong with the wording of
    of this rather long and involved
    question?

168 What could the 'W' stand for in the following: H D S on
    a W?
    a)Wombat b)Wall c)Wish d)Watch

169 What is the total of: Legs of a horse plus legs of a bird plus limbs of Long John Silver?
a)9 b)10 c)8 d)15

MORE QUICKIES

Tricky little questions to try out on your friends.

170 What day comes after 27 February?
a) 28 February b)1 March c)29 February

171 How old could somebody born in 1893 have been in 1899?
a)90 b)5 c)4

172 What letters come between 'a' and 'b' in the alphabet?
a)c b)d c)lpha

173 A brick is four inches longer than it is thick. If it is not very thick how long is it?
a)5 inches b)4 inches c)3 inches

174 Sir W. S. Churchill's Christian names were Winston and Spencer, what was his surname?
a)Archibald b)Churchill c)Marmaduke d)Prime Minister

175 If a double-headed coin comes down head first, what will it come down next time?
a)Heads b)Tails

176 If John's twin is twelve on Tuesday, how old will John be?
a)54 b)Albert c)12

177 Paul Gimbelbrackett's mother remarried his father's uncle, what should Paul now call her?
a)Great-aunt b)Aunt c)Mrs Currywinkle d)Mum

178 Is the day after tomorrow week the same as yesterday fortnight?
a)Yes b)No

179 What is the French for 'L'amour'?
a)Dorothy b)Love c)L'amour

180 Here is some wire netting, how many strands of wire are there?

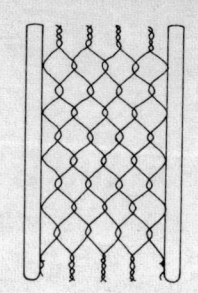

a)8 b)4 c)16 d)9

181 A view of a table from the top and the side.

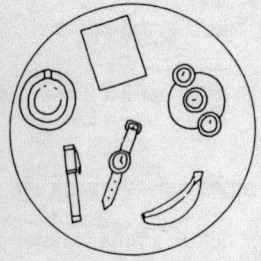

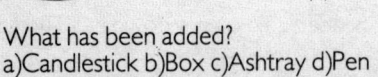

What has been added?
a)Candlestick b)Box c)Ashtray d)Pen

182 In the drawing below Tom and Beryl are facing the same way, Steve and Beryl are on each other's left, which one is Anna?

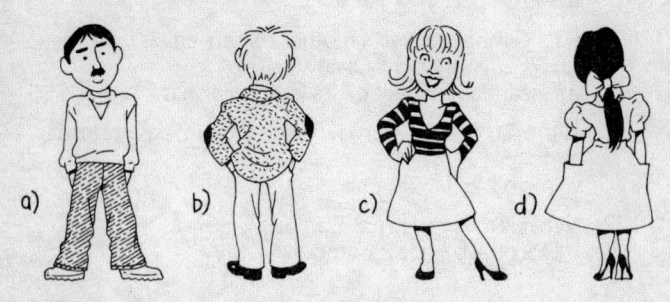

a) b) c) d)

38

183   Here is a set of vases:

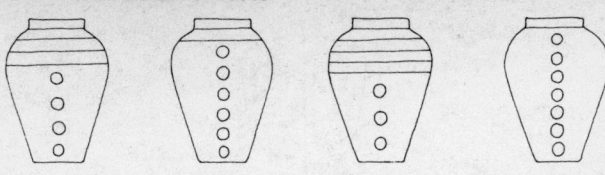

Which of the vases below is missing from the set?

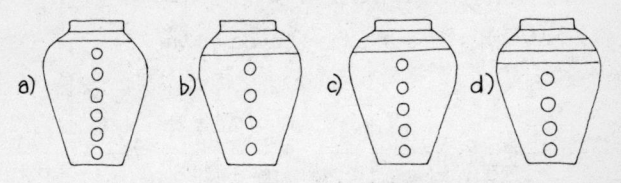

a)   b)   c)   d)

184   Spot the difference between the two pictures?

185   How many pieces of string are shown below?

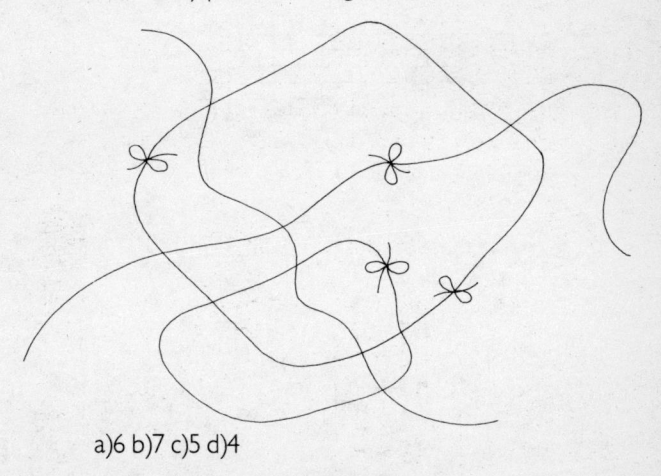

a)6 b)7 c)5 d)4

186

Which is the same shield upside-down?

a) b) c) d)

187 These A/W— shapes interlock as shown

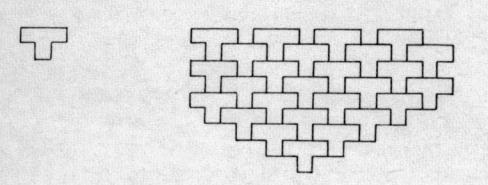

Which of these shapes do not interlock?

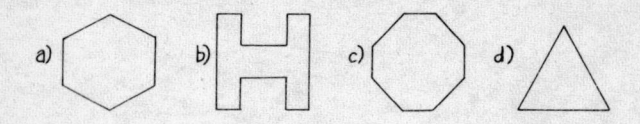

a) b) c) d)

188 Here are three encyclopedias of 100 pages each excluding covers:

How many pages are there between the first entry of 'O' and the last entry of 'Z', excluding covers? (There are no endpapers.)
a)100 b)200 c)0 d)300

189 A fire trapped poor Peter and Mary on the fifteenth floor, so they both jumped out of the window. Unfortunately Mary was seriously hurt, but Peter landed safely on the concrete path below. Neither of them was carrying anything. How did Peter survive without a bruise or a scratch?

190 There is a matchbox lid and an orange on a table. Is it possible to push the orange through the matchbox lid without breaking or distorting either?
a)Yes b)No

191 Detective Dodds has a speech impediment. This was his report of a murder: 'The murger took place in the pong in the gargen, the bogy was found in the mug, and I Getective Goggs know who gig it.' What was the detective's speech impediment?
a)All g's he pronounced as d's b)All d's he pronounced as g's c)He has a lisp d)He mostly pronounces d's as g's

192 At a reunion for old soldiers, four of them had only one leg, six of the others had only one arm, and of the other ten, who had all their limbs, five had sticks. How many old soldiers were there at the reunion?
a)30 b)70 c)20 d)10

193 I can make one new candle from the wax left over after burning three candles. If I buy 13 candles, how many will I be able to burn altogether?
a)16 b)17 c)18 d)19

OBSERVATION FOUR... THE ART GALLERY

Study all the pictures and signs in this strange art gallery for just thirty seconds, and then turn over the page and test your powers of observation.

43

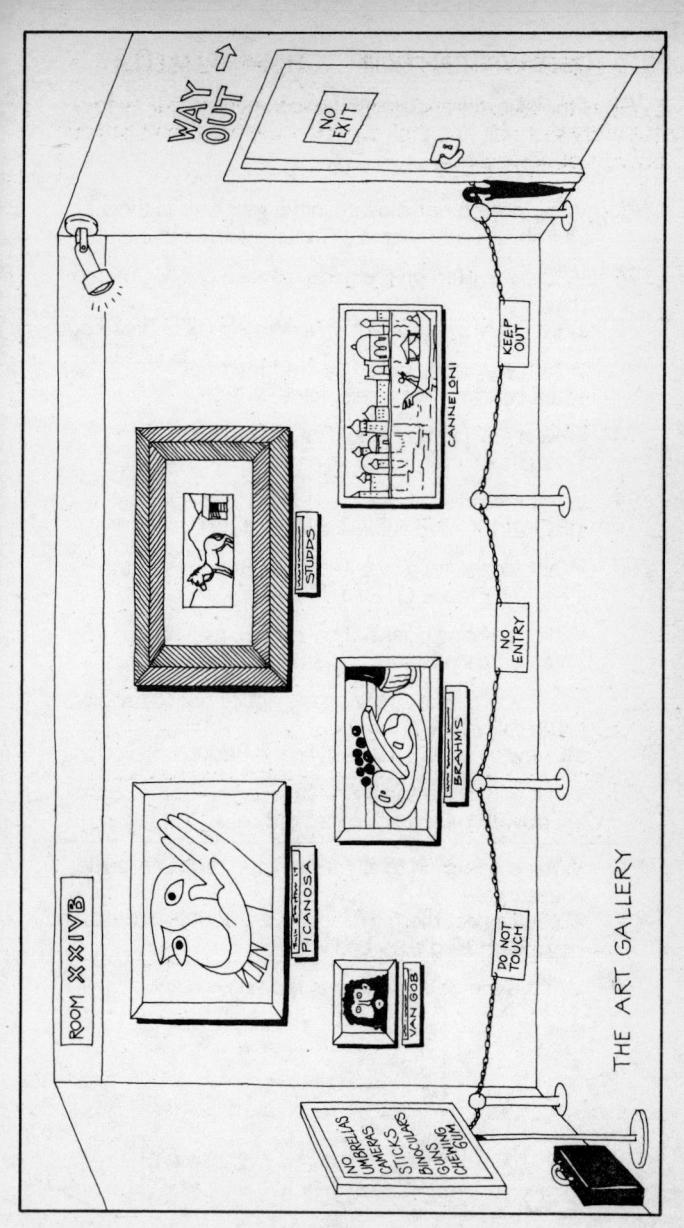

OBSERVATION FOUR... THE ART GALLERY

What details have you managed to remember?

194 What is the room number?
a)XXIVB b)25B c)XXXVIB d)XXVA

195 What object, not allowed in the gallery, is in there?
a)Umbrella b)Briefcase c)Camera d)Newspaper

196 What is written on the middle notice hanging on the chain?
a)No Entry b)Keep Out c)No Way In d)Do Not Touch

197 Which way is the horse by Studds facing?
a)Left b)Right c)It's an elephant

198 How many posts are holding up the chain?
a)4 b)3 c)6

199 What is written above the door?
a)ROOM XXIVB b)EXIT c)WAY OUT

200 Which of the following items is in Brahms's picture?
a)Hand b)House c)Table d)Boat

201 Which painting does not have a title plate under it?
a)Van Gob's b)Brahms's c)Studds's d)Canneloni's

202 What was the last thing on the notice board prohibited in the gallery?
a)Chewing Gum b)Guns c)Tennis Rackets d)Clothing

203 What was in the top right-hand corner of the room?
a)Cobweb b)Lamp c)Notice d)Bird

---

204 What is common to all these things: cabbage, kettle, cheese, cake?
a)You can eat them b)They have a double letter c)They begin with 'C' d)they end with 'e'

205 What is the next diagram in this sequence?

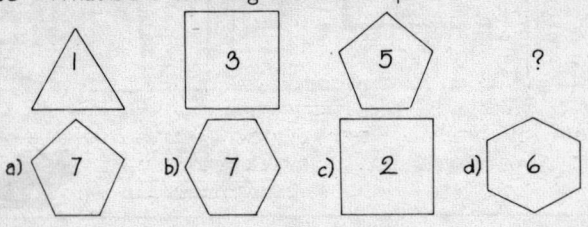

△1 □3 ⬠5 ?

a) ⬠7   b) ⬡7   c) □2   d) ⬡6

44

206 What bird occurs in each of these places: Finchley, Winchelsea, Hitchen and Sheen?
a)Burrow's finch b)Sparrowhawk c)Hen d)Dodo

207 If CALM is to CLAM: what is SOWN to?
a)SNOW b)SWAN c)SWON d)NOWS

208 Which letter occurs most in this nursery rhyme?
Hickory dickory dock,
The mouse ran up the clock
The clock struck one
The mouse ran down,
Hickory dickory dock.
a)C b)O c)K d)E

209 Which of the following can a man not marry?
a)His sister's sister-in-law b)His widow's cousin c)His nephew's widow d)His mother-in-law's niece

210 Which came first, BBC1 or BBC2?
a)BBC1 b)BBC2 c)Both at the same time

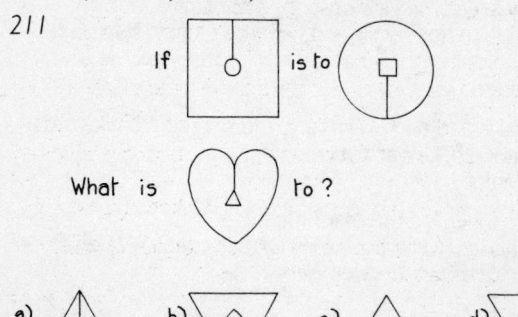

211 If [square with circle] is to [circle with square], What is [heart with triangle] to?
a) [triangle with heart] b) [inverted triangle with heart] c) [triangle with square] d) [inverted triangle with heart]

212 I live on the odd numbered side of a street at number 7, my friend lives at number 27. How many houses are there between us?
a)9 b)10 c)20 d)19

213 What do you think the Spanish word 'cigarra', which gives us the word cigar, means?
a)A cicada, an insect that looks like a cigar b)The Indian word for tobacco c)A tube d)A crayfish, native to Cuba, which is known to smoke tobacco

214 In which direction do you turn a screw to tighten it?
a)Clockwise b)Counter-clockwise

215 Which of these methods of communication is the most direct?
a)Telephone b)Television c)Semaphore d)All the same

216 How many eggs does a peacock lay?
a)0 b)1 c)2 d)4

217 Lots of different things are numbered for size. Which of the things below is the odd one out because of its numbering?
a)Shoes b)Knitting needles c)Dresses d)Hats

QUICKIES AGAIN

218 How many pop records get into the top fifty every week?
a)6 b)277 c)50

219 Why are some girls described as being auburn?
a)They're not very good with fire extinguishers b)It's the colour of their hair c)Their mother's name is Blondee

220 If dad is dad backwards and mum is mum backwards, what is a backward you?
a)Mentally deficient b)ouy c)uoy

221 Who invented the mackintosh?
a)Charles Mackintosh b)Arfur Raincoat b)Walter Proof d)Sir Charlton Dardenelle

222 How many P's in a pod?
a)1 b)6 c)8

223 If Bobby was born two years after Tommy, how much older is Bobby than Tommy?
a)2 years b)2 months c)He isn't older

224 What is the female peacock called?
a)Elizabeth b)Peahen c)Peewit d)Old bean

225 What cheese is named after Cheddar Gorge?
a)Gorge-onzola b)Cheshire c)Cheddar

226 What sound does a cuckoo make?
a)Cock-a-doodle-doo b)Cuckoo c)Gowk d)Cheep

227 Which river flows between the banks of the Nile?
a)Egypt b)Tigris c)Nile d)Blue Nile

228 What does a normal household electric plug look like?
Try and decide from memory, not by picking one up.

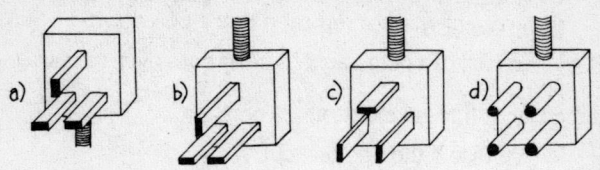

229 How many pence in an Irish pound?
a)100 b)87 c)90 d)10

230 There are twice as many odd-numbered houses on
one side of a street as there are even-numbered
houses on the other. If all the houses are equally
spaced, what number is opposite number 9?
a)10 b)8 c)6 d)2

231 Nosmo King was a famous comedian a few years ago.
Why did he call himself that name?
a)His father was Mr Joe King b)His real name was
Nismo Kong c)He split a 'No Smoking' notice in two
d)He was fat

232 What is the maximum number of similar-sized circular
coins, placed flat on a table, that can touch the edge of
one other coin of the same size?
a)5 b)6 c)8 d)10

233 If Terry Wogan is Tewo and Margaret Thatcher is
Matha, who is Roba?
a)Rabbie Burns b)Jason Robarts c)Ronnie Barker
d)Richard Baker

234 Which is not an anagram of a girl's name?
a)Yam b)Yak c)Yiv d)Yob

235 Two boys share some equal-sized cakes. One boy eats
one and then they share the rest. One of them has now
had three times as much as the other. How many cakes
did they have to start with?
a)21 b)2 c)9 d)3

236 If London is to Donegal, what is Bristol to?
a)Belfast b)Londonderry c)Bootle d)Tolpuddle

237 A car travelling down a busy hill at over 60 miles per hour came to an abrupt stop. The car behind, which had been travelling at the same speed, hit it. Although there was considerable damage, nobody was hurt and the accident was not reported to the police, why?

238 What part of a pole-vaulter's body goes over the bar first?
a)Hands b)Head c)Bottom d)Feet

239 Which vase is the odd one out?

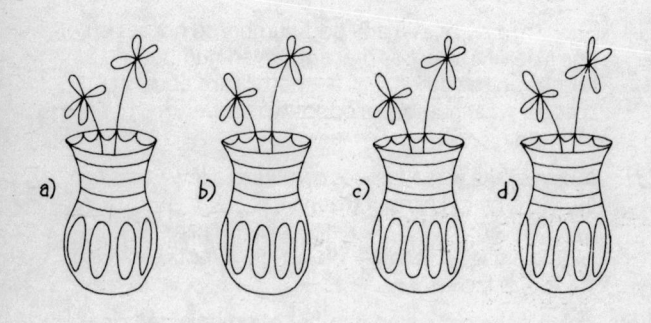

240 What is the next number in the sequence below?
8 5 4 9 1 7 ?
a)6 b)10 c)3 d)2

241 Newspapers are usually made of large sheets folded in two, so that each sheet has four pages of the paper. In a 12-page paper what page is on the back of page 4 as well as page 3?
a)7 b)10 c)9 d)5

242 Although it was at night and dense fog, Tom was able to give a signal of warning to deaf Dan, who was in grave danger in a boat two miles offshore. How did he do it without the use of any equipment?

243 Here is a beautiful painting by the famous artist, Dino Daubi, what does it show?

a)A polar bear on the ice b)A black market in daytime
c)A cloudy sky at night d)A black cat sitting on a fence

244 Shown below are two views of a pile of coins, one from the top and one from the side. Could they be the same pile?

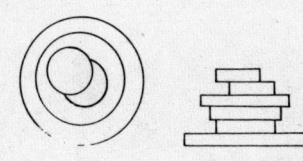

a)Yes b)No

245 Three boys and five girls sit round a round table. What is the most number of girls who do not have to sit next to a boy?
a)5 b)3 c)2

246 In cricket a batsman hits and runs 3 runs. But the fielder's return goes over the boundary for 4, the batsmen run one more. How many runs have been scored?
a)3 b)4 c)7 d)8

247 Where did the welly boot gets its name?
a)The Welsh rubber boot b)The Duke of Wellington
c)The Town of Wells d)Old Norse word to wallow

248 What shape are dice?
a)Spherical b)Duodecahedronical c)Conical d)Cubic

OBSERVATION FIVE ... THE COUNTRY

Another scene for you to study for thirty seconds and then answer the questions over the page.

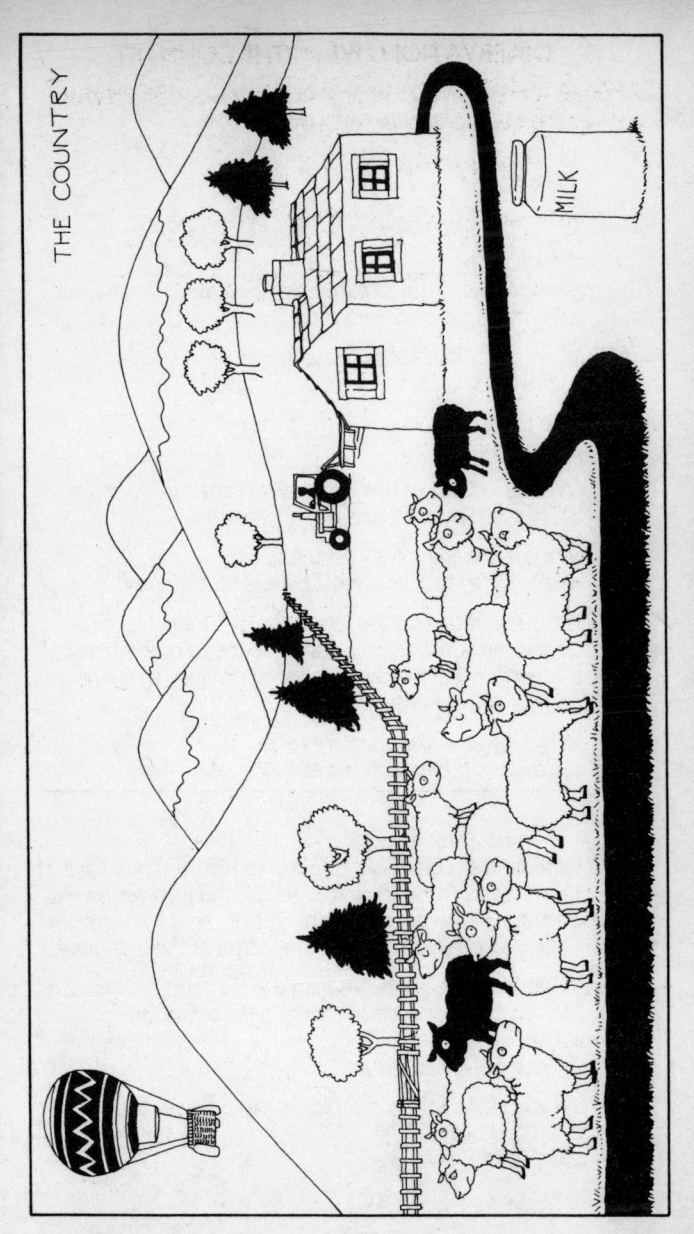

THE COUNTRY

OBSERVATION FIVE... THE COUNTRY

249 What is on the other side of the road to the sheep?
a)Milk churn b)Gate c)House d)Haystack

250 How many sheep are facing left?
a)3 b)8 c)6

251 How many windows are there in the house?
a)2 b)3 c)1

252 Which side of the picture does the path come from?
a)Left b)Right c)Bottom

253 How many black sheep are there?
a)2 b)1 c)3

254 Are there any people in the picture?
a)Yes b)No

255 What is on top of three of the mountains?
a)Trees b)Snow c)Sheep d)A man

256 Where is the chimney on the house?
a)Left b)Right c)Centre d)There is no chimney

257 Is the mountain on the left of the picture in front, behind or at the same distance as the one on the right?
a)Nearer b)Further away c)Same distance d)There is no mountain on the left

258 Which type of tree is there most of?
a)Conifers b)Deciduous trees c)Equal

---

259 I am driving a bus from London to Bristol. There are 21 passengers. At Reading five get off and two get on. At Swindon three get off and six get on. At Bath eight get off and five get on. What is the name of the bus driver?

260 What have Boudicca, William the Conqueror, Horatio Nelson and Florence Nightingale in common?
a)They're women b)They're royal c)They're dead d)They only had one arm

261 Which of the following colours can be associated with the word bottle?
a)Pink b)Yellow c)Blue

262 Is it possible to stand with your heels against a wall of a room and touch your toes with your hands? Try it.
a)Yes b)No

263 Ellen is 5 years old, David is 4 years old and Josephine is 10 years old; how old is Alan?
a)5 b)3 c)1 d)8

264 Which of these is a new moon?

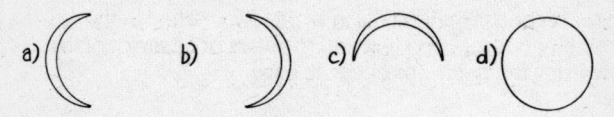

a) (b)) c) ⌒ d) ○

265 If TRAP is to PART, what is OASIS to?
a)SISAO b)SISOA c)SOASI d)ISSAO

MORE QUICKIES

266 What fruit is mainly used in the making of raspberry jam?
a)Lemons b)Apples c)Raspberries

267 How many legs does each contestant have in a three-legged race?
a)Three b)Four c)Two d)One-and-a-half

268 Who was not involved in the Franco–Prussian War?
a)The French b)The Prussians c)General Franco

269 What shape is a circle?
a)Round b)Square c)Shipshape

270 Who crewed for Clare Francis in her solo trip round the world?
a)Francis Chichester b)She did c)Her crewman

271 On what day of the week will next year's Good Friday fall?
a)Easter b)Sunday c)Monday d)Friday

272 If you were doing a handstand, which would be nearest your chin?
a)Your nose b)Your mouth c)Your navel

273 Which of the following words rhyme with 'go'?
a)Cow b)Bow c)Bough

274 What animal has big feet, tusks and a trunk?
a)Elk b)Electrician c)Elephant

275 Which weighs most?
a)Two pounds of feathers b)One pound of gold
c)Neither d)Both the same

OBSERVATION SIX ... THE PLANT-POT

Thirty seconds again to take in all the information in the picture opposite. Then test your powers of observation by answering the questions over the page.

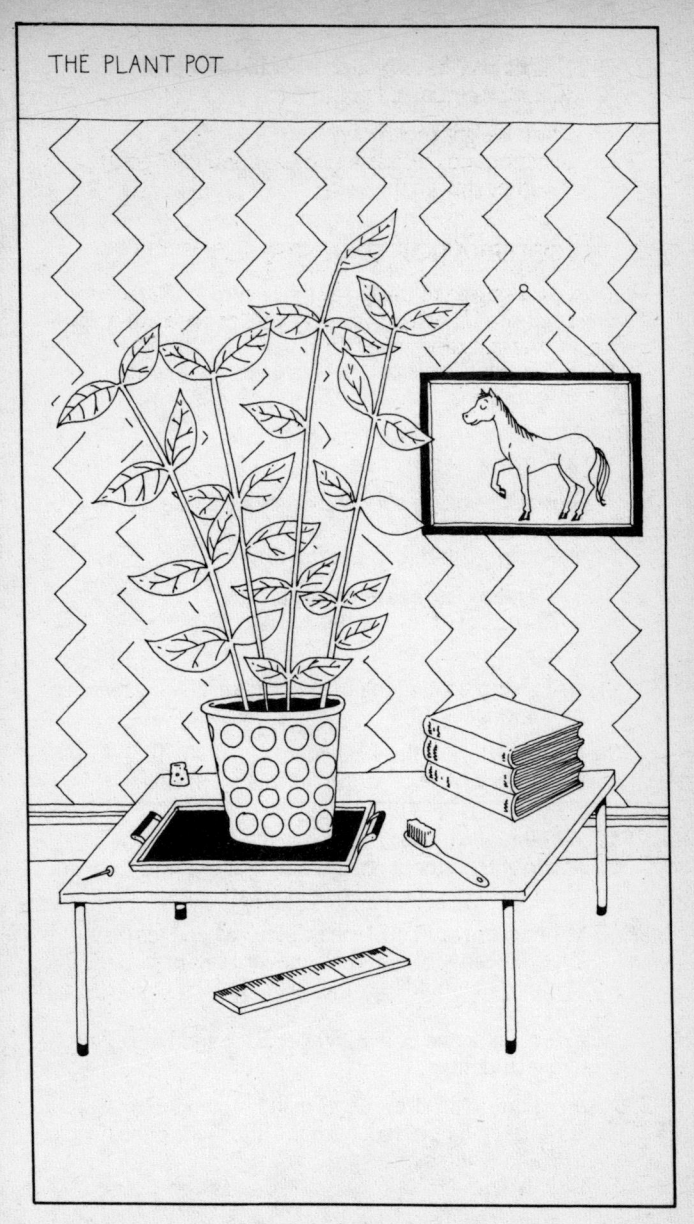

THE PLANT POT

OBSERVATION SIX... THE PLANT-POT

276 What is the pattern on the plant-pot?
a)Circles b)Plain c)Wavy lines

277 How many books are on the table?
a)2 b)3 c)4 d)1

278 What is under the table?
a)Dog b)Ruler c)Mat d)Shoe

279 What is in the picture on the wall?
a)Another plant b)A dog c)A horse

280 How many leaves do not have veins in them?
a)1 b)2 c)3 d)4

281 What is the plant-pot standing on?
a)Tray b)Mat c)Frisbee

282 Besides books, a cork and a nail, what else is on the table?
a)Toothbrush b)Cup c)Screwdriver

283 How many leaves are on the plant?
a)20 b)25 c)30

284 Is the table:
a)Higher than it is long b)Lower than it is long c)As high as it is long

285 What pattern is the wallpaper?
a)Zigzags b)Vertical stripes c)Flowers d)Circles

---

286 A cowboy rode into a town on Friday and stayed there four nights, without going anywhere else. He rode out again on Friday. How did he do that?

287 Whenever I say 'red' I mean 'blue', whenever I say 'blue' I mean 'white' and whenever I say 'black' I mean 'red'. What would I say the colours of the Union Jack are?
a)Red, Black and Blue b)White, Black and Blue c)Red, White and Blue

288 A man, who can lift greater than his own weight, stands in a bucket. By pulling on a rope attached to the handle, is he able to lift himself up?
a)No b)Yes

289 Without buckets, ropes, pulleys or any other equipment, how can anybody lift themselves into the air?

290 Where do you find 3 opposite 0, and 1 opposite 8?
a) Lifts b) Calendars c) Calculators d) Telephone dials

291 In which of the following is there not a dog hiding?
a) Darlington b) Dragon c) Devonport d) Dingo

292 Which bolt below locks this sliding door?

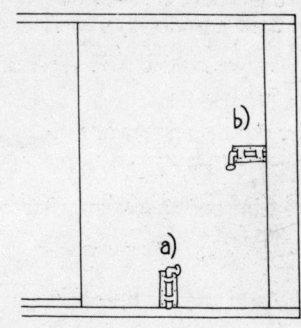

a) b) c) Both d) Neither

293 What is the next figure in this sequence?

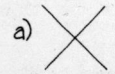

294 In the sum below a sign is missing, what is it?
5 5 + 2 = 3
a) + b) − c) × d) ÷

295 My first is in Eric but not in Clive
My second is in Donny but not in Wendy
My third is in Fred but not in Geoffrey
Who am I?
a) Roger b) Vic c) Rob d) Rod

296 A motorist was driving down a narrow country lane. His car lights were not working, there were no street lamps and no moonlight. Yet he still managed to avoid running into a nun dressed all in black walking away from him down the centre of the road, how?

297 STAR-SPAR-SEAR-SEAT-FEAT-FRET-FREE-TREE-TREK What word is missing?
a)SPAT b)FEAR c)FEET d)SEEK

298 A pair of rabbits have six baby rabbits every six months, each of the babies has six babies after they are six months old. How many rabbits could there be after 13 months?
a)36 b)44 c)86 d)344

299 What sport is a jewel with half a horse inside it?
a)Shooting b)Hockey c)Rugby d)Pearl Diving

300 What is the difference between twice twenty-two and twice two plus twenty?
a)20 b)2 c)22

301 Which is the odd one out here?
a)KT b)LN c)LC d)NV

302 One leg of a table is 1cm short. You have a number of blocks which are either 3cm or 5cm thick. How many do you need to put under the legs of the table to level it up?
a)1 b)3 c)5 d)7

303 If you think of a number, double it twice and then divide by the number you first thought of, what are you left with?
a)4 b)0 c)13 d)2

304 Beansprouts increase their height by exactly half as much again each day. If they are picked today when they are six inches tall, how high were they at the same time yesterday?
a)4 inches b)3 inches c)2 inches d)Not enough information

305 Fred, while asleep on a chair with his feet up on a table, accidentally and unintentionally killed Rosemary. When he woke up he found her dead on the floor by his feet, and the carpet all wet. How had it happened?

306 If [figure] is to [figure]

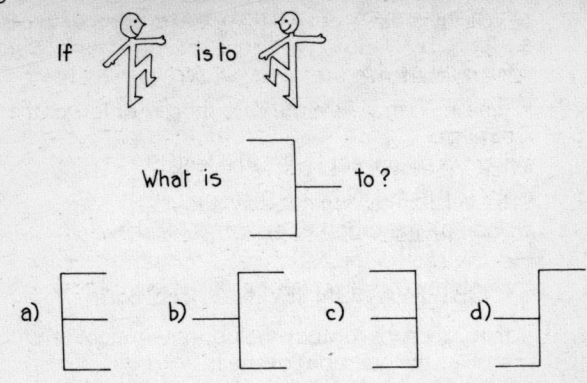

What is [⊢] to?

a) [⊢ shape] b) [⊣ shape] c) [⊣ shape] d) [⊢ shape]

307 What is the next letter in sequence?
D N O S A J ?
a) J b) F c) C d) L

308 Are there more triangles or squares in the diagram below?

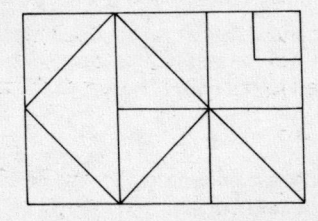

a) Triangles b) Squares c) The same

309 A motorist, approaching some traffic lights on red, didn't stop and tore across the junction, mounted the pavement and ended up inside the front of a sweetshop. A policeman witnessed the whole thing but did nothing to arrest the motorist, and was quite right not to do so, why?

310 A farmer had two haystacks in one corner of a field and three haystacks in another. If he put them all together, how many haystacks would he have?
a) 5 b) 2 c) 1

311 A box is half as deep as it is wide, and half as wide as it is high. How many of such boxes do you need to make a cube?
a)4 b)8 c)12 d)16

312 In June in Australia are the days shorter or longer than the nights?
a)Shorter b)Longer c)The same length

313 What relation can we not do without?
a)Uncle b)Grandmother c)Sister d)Nephew

OBSERVATION SEVEN ... THE BUS

Another thirty seconds to study the opposite picture carefully and then answer the questions overleaf.

THE BUS

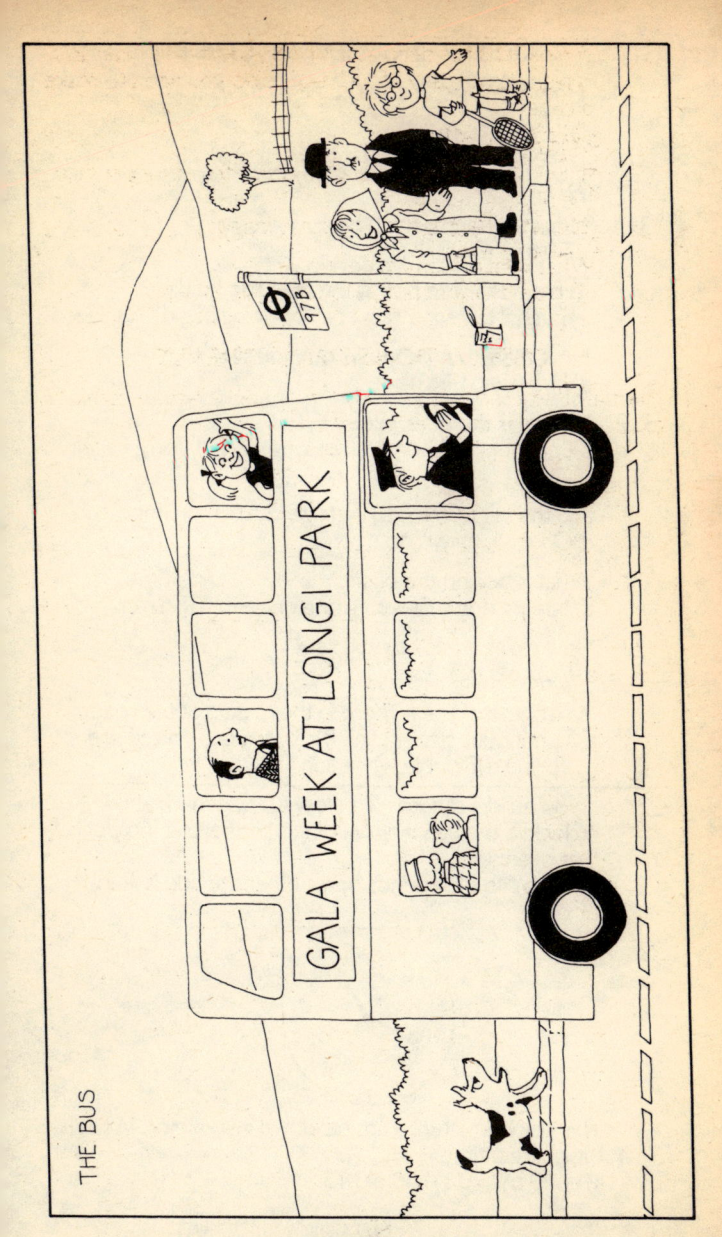

OBSERVATION SEVEN... THE BUS

314 How many people are in the picture?
a)5 b)7 c)8 d)10

315 Is the driver of the bus wearing a cap?
a)Yes b)No

316 What number is the bus?
a)90A b)97 c)97B

317 What is the little boy at the bus stop holding?
a)Satchel b)Tennis racket c)Shopping bag d)Dog's lead

318 How many bus windows can you see?
a)11 b)12 c)14 d)15

319 Where is the 'Gala Week'?
a)Longhurst b)Long Park c)Longi Park d)Lonig Park

320 Where is the bus?
a)In the High Street b)Trafalgar Square c)Timbuktu d)On a country road

321 What is behind the bus?
a)Barking dog b)Sleeping dog c)Sheep d)Tin can

322 How many trees can you see?
a)1 b)2 c)3 d)5

323 What type of line is there in the middle of the road?
a)Continuous straight line b)Continuous dotted line c)No line d)Double white line

---

324 If you build a sandcastle below full tide mark at 7 o'clock in the morning, will it still be there at 7 o'clock that evening?
a)Yes b)No c)Depends on whether the tide is going in or out

325

This clock is pictured upside-down in a mirror. What is the correct time?
a)11.20 b)7.10 c)4.50 d)3.15

326 Eleven has six, one has three, how many does four have?
a)9 b)4 c)2 d)1

327 A snail climbing up a 7-metre wall counteracts gravity and slipperiness and covers 3 metres in one hour. It then rests for an hour, during which time the natural forces against it make it slip back 2 metres. It continues this progress until it reaches the top of the wall after nine hours. Resting at the top for an hour, it decides to come down again. How long does it take to reach the bottom?
a)1 hour b)2 hours c)2 hours 20 minutes d)3 hours

328 If the letters A–Z are represented by the numbers 1–26 in order, which of the following words would have the lowest value?
a)FIG b)CAT c)DECK d)MOP

329 The initial letters of the words in the first line of a well-known nursery rhyme are 'T B M T B M', what is it?

330 And here is another: 'L J H S I A C'. What nursery rhyme is that?

MORE TRICKY QUICKIES

331 How often does a monthly periodical come out?
a)Yearly b)On 3 January c)Every month

332 How many times a day does the sun rise?
a)2 b)1 c)0

333 What animal has tusks and lives in the sea?
a)Elephant b)Dolphin c)Shark d)Walrus

334 Where are you standing if you can only look south?
a)North Pole b)South Pole c)John O'Groats

335 What has a duck-billed platypus got that no other mammal has?
a)A pouch b)Teats c)Eggs d)A duck-bill

336 Who wrote the Strauss Waltzes?
a)Johann Stroud b)Richard Waltz c)Johann Strauss d)Engelbert Strauss

337 What is half of nothing?
a)Nothing b)Minus a half c)Half

338 Where would you expect to find an arctic fox?
a)France b)Woolworths c)The Arctic

339 Which of these furry things is not an animal?
a)Furry bear b)Furry caterpillar c)Pussy d)Pussy willow

340 What do Eskimos always write in?
a)Pencil b)The snow c)Hebrew d)Eskimo

341 Which letter is South-west of the X?

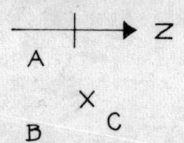

342 A branch of a tree grew three new branches last year, and each branch grew three branches this year, how many branches are there?
a)9 b)12 c)13 d)16

343 What do these words have in common: BOW ALTHOUGH PHARAOH BUREAU NO?
a)They all have an O in them b)They rhyme c)They are nouns

344

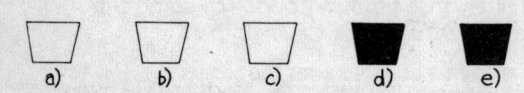

Which glass should you move to get the glasses alternately full and empty?

345 What word has 'pea' been substituted for in the sentence: 'A peace of peaty peasants came peath and peaaged pea a peatnight in the peaceful peaests of Peat William'.
a)Fen b)Sin c)Spa d)For

346 What is the only letter you can replace each of the letters in the word TEAM with, and each time make a new word?
a)S b)H c)B d)R

347 What do these letters C O P S U V X have in common?
a) Roman numerals b) All small forms are written above the line c) Same shape capitals as small d) All curved letters

348

Three ladies wear different coloured hats. Lady 'a' looking to her left can see a red hat. Lady 'c' looking to her right can see a yellow hat. Lady 'b' is not wearing a red hat. Who is wearing the red hat?

349 I,V,X,L,C,D,M are Roman numerals for 1,5,10,50,100,500,1000 respectively. What happened in the last year represented by just one each of those numerals, the year MDCLXVI?
a) Battle of Hastings b) Magna Carta c) Fire of London d) Four-minute mile

350 If M is to W, what is p to?
a) D b) d c) b d) X

351 The sun rises in the east in the Northern Hemisphere. In which direction does it set in the Southern Hemisphere?
a) East b) West c) South

352 You get in a lift at the sixth floor of a ten-storey building and go down to the basement. How many floors do you pass by?
a) 5 b) 9 c) 6 d) 7

353 What would you think would be an appropriate career for careful Carl Carter?
a) Cameraman b) Computer Programmer c) Car salesman c) Sewer cleaner

354 Which is the next triangle in this sequence:

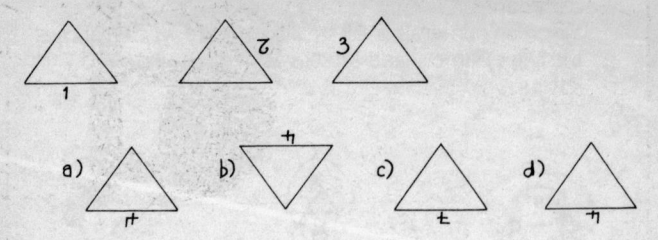

OBSERVATION EIGHT ... THE BOOKSHELF

Take a good detailed look at this picture for at least thirty seconds and then turn the page and test your powers of observation.

THE BOOKSHELF

OBSERVATION EIGHT... THE BOOKSHELF

355 Which elephant book-end has its trunk raised?
a)The one on the left b)The one on the right

356 Which book should you look in to find out where Hungary is?
a)The tallest book b)The one on the right c)The one on the left

357 How many books are there?
a)6 b)10 c)9 d)8

358 In which order are the puzzle books?
a)3 1 2 b)3 2 1 c)1 3 2 d)1 2 3

359 What language do the people of France speak?
a)Spanish b)Asian c)French

360 How many books have verses in them?
a)1 b)2 c)0

361 Which is the fattest book on the shelf?
a)The Atlas b)The Dictionary c)The Bible

362 How many books have a 'P' in the title?
a)2 b)6 c)All of them

363 Which way are the elephants facing?
a)Left b)Right

364 How many of the elephants have tusks?
a)2 b)1 c)0

---

365 If Penny is to Penelope, who is Peggy to?
a)Pegelope b)Margaret c)Priscilla d)Megan

366 If SPOT is to OPTS, what is TARN to?
a)NART b)RANT c)TRAM d)ARNT

367 What is the difference between half a dozen baker's dozens and half a dozen dozens?
a)A dozen b)A baker c)Half a dozen

368 What is the difference between a ton of opals and a ton of soap?
a)Half a ton b)Suds c)L d)61

369 To win the noughts and crosses game below you have to get four in a row:

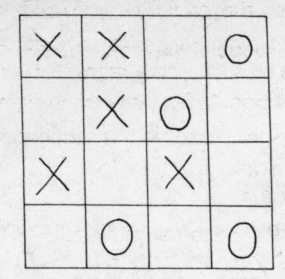

Will the person playing noughts win with their next play or not?
a) Win b) Lose c) Draw

370 What is the least number of coins you need to pay for something that costs 77p?
a) 4 b) 6 c) 1

371 As I was walking to St Ives,
I met a man with seven wives,
Each wife had seven sons in tow,
And each son a child did carry so.
How many persons were definitely going to St Ives?
a) 106 b) 56 c) 1 d) 57

372 From a bag of sweets Alan took ¼. Then Bob took ⅓ of the remainder. Clive then took ½ of what was left, and finally Dave took the remaining three. How many did Alan take?
a) 3 b) 4 c) 6 d) 24

373 The Roman numeral for ten is X, so what is half of ten?
a) 5 b) I c) ½ d) L

374

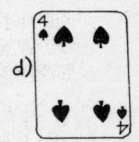

What card is next to the one that is two away from the one on the left of the end one?

375 The number 19 can of course be divided by 19, but what other whole number can be divided into it?
a)9 b)7 c)1

376 Every year a plant divides its stalk into two. After six years it has 64 stalks, how many stalks did it start with?
a)1 b)2 c)32

377 What is the next letter in this sequence?
S M T W T F ?
a)M b)S c)U

378 What can you not live without for more than three days in the Sahara?
a)Water b)Clothes c)Food d)Air

379 How many letter A's are there in the numbers from 1 to 12?
a)0 b)1 c)4

380 The names Otto, Anna and Eve have something in common with one of the following names, which?
a)Emma b)Hannah c)Emil d)Leon

381

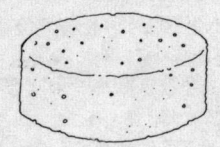

What is the least number of straight cuts needed to cut this cake into eight equal portions?
a)8 b)4 c)3 d)2

382 What part of your body can you not see, even if you use a single mirror?
a)Back of your ear b)Sole of your foot c)Your eyelid d)Small of your back

383 If all insects were a hundred times bigger, which of the following would be the biggest?
a)Flea b)Ladybird c)Dragonfly

384 Which way does the Queen's head face on a 10p coin? Don't look in your pocket or money-box until you've answered!
a)Left b)Right c)Straight out

385 Which is the odd square out?

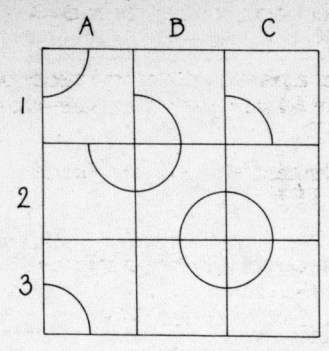

a)A3 b)B2 c)C1

TRICKY QUICKIES

386 What day comes before Shrove Tuesday?
a)Ash Wednesday b)Whitsun c)Monday

387 How often does a perennial flower, flower?
a)Once a year b)Once every three years c)Never

388 Where did the Battle of Hastings take place?
a)Waterloo b)Battle c)Nuneaton

389 Who is my father's only son?
a)My sister's son b)My brother's father c)My son's father

390 What is the poem 'Ode to a Nightingale' about?
a)A night in jail b)A nightingale c)A knight in shining armour

391 What do roses smell of?
a)Manure b)Fish c)Vindaloo curry d)Roses

392 How many matches are there in an empty matchbox?
a)None b)Half as many as before c)One less than when there were two

393 How many months have 30 days in them?
a)11 b)4 c)6

394 What is the furthest a man can jump?
a)29 feet 6½ inches b)7 feet 5 inches c)Over 12 miles

395 What is the language spoken by a woman from Denmark?
a)Filthy b)Dutch c)Manspeak d)Danish

396 Will this rope form a knot or not if both ends are pulled together?
a)Yes b)No

397 Which of these words is unlike the other three?
a)Ponder b)Afghan c)Stuart d)Hijack

398 How many times between 12 noon and 12 midnight are the minute and hour hands of a clock directly opposite each other?
a)10 b)11 c)12 d)24

399 Only one of these pieces is not the same shape as all the others, which?

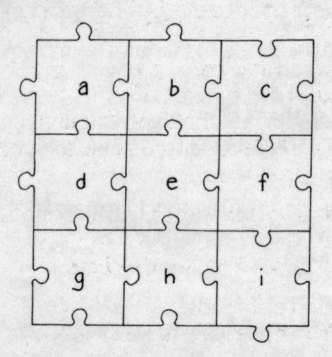

400 If you crossed the International Date Line going west, would you:
a)Lose a day b)Lose weight c)Gain a day d)Gain two days?

401 What national park is Mount Snowdon in?
a)Wales National Park b)Beddgelert c)Snowdonia d)Margate

402 A comb has 30 teeth, excluding the outside ones, how many gaps are there between the teeth?
a)31 b)30 c)29

403 What is the least number of cubes pictured below?

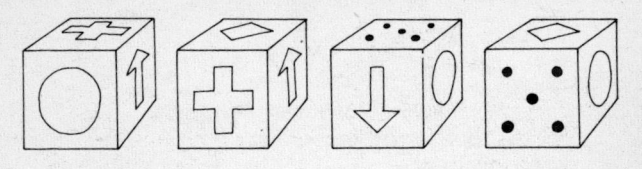

a)1 b)2 c)3 d)4

404 David is the half-brother of Pat, but Pat is not the half-brother of David. How is that possible?
a)Pat is David's cousin b)Pat is a girl c)Pat is his brother

405 Which country in the world has the wrong capital at its centre?
a)Australia b)Guatemala c)Czechoslovakia d)Ecuador

406 Intelligent life on the planet Orng is divided into three types of being. Verties who always tell the truth, Faffies who always lie and Obods who tell the truth and lie alternately.
An Obod said: 'I am red.'
A Vertie said: 'Faffies are blue.'
A Faffie said: 'I am not the same colour as an Obod.'
An Obod said: 'We are all the same colour.'
What colour are Obods?

407 Where would you expect to find a relation stuck in a heavy weight?
a)France b)Kitchen c)Jupiter d)Taunton

408 Who invented diamonds?
a)South Africa b)Neil Diamond c)Nobody

409 Who is hidden in 37 Drainpipe Terrace?
a)A plumber b)Ian c)Peter d)A wallaby

OBSERVATION NINE ... TINS

Look carefully at these tins for thirty seconds and then answer the questions over the page.

TINS

OBSERVATION NINE... TINS

410 How many tins besides the Irish Stew tin are open?
a)3 b)2 c)1 d)0

411 How many tins of Baked Beans are there?
a)2 b)3 c)4

412 What was in the only non-cylindrical tin?
a)Anchovies b)Tuna c)Irish Stew d)Fried Frogs Legs

413 What letter can you not see from 'Tomato Soup'?
a)T b)P c)O

414 What stands to the immediate left of the blank tin?
a)Baked Beans b)Peas c)Irish Stew d)Chocolate-covered Ants

415 What is above the peas?
a)Nothing b)Peaches c)Pears d)Peas

416 How many containers are there?
a)10 b)11 c)9 d)12

417 What does the tallest tin contain?
a)Honeyed Grubs b)Tomato Soup c)Peaches d)Tuna

418 Besides the sauce bottle, what else is not a tin?
a)Tin opener b)Knife c)Salt-cellar d)Orange

419 Which tin does not have a label?
a)Anchovies b)Clotted Cream c)Tuna d)Blank tin

---

420 What is missing from this poem if all the others are in it?
A Jack-in-the-Box has a spring
Which quickly dumps him out
But lazy boys can never bring
Themselves to jump about

421 You have two leaky 5-litre buckets, which both lose all their contents over five minutes. Carrying one bucket in each hand you are unable to stop them leaking. How much water would you be able to put on a fire which takes you exactly five minutes to get to from the tap?
a)None b)5 litres c)1 litre d)2½ litres

422 What shape do the three pieces below make when fitted together?

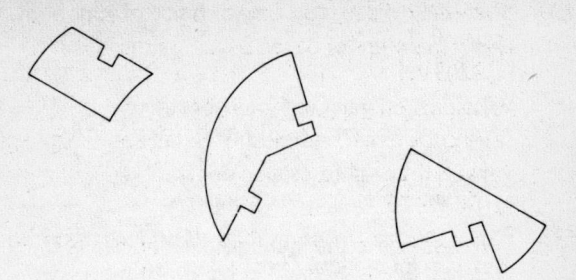

a)Semicircle b)Circle c)Oval d)Square

423 The defendant said he was not at the scene of the crime because he never went to the bank on any day that did not have an S in it. He was lying, so was he at the crime which took place on Monday?
a)Yes b)No c)Can't tell

424 If you lie on your back with your feet facing south, which way should you turn to look east?
a)Left b)Right

425 If reviver is to reviver, what is river to?
a)Verir b)Reriv c)Liver d)River

426 Where do doors have their handles?
a)Opposite side to the hinges b)Same side as the hinges c)On the outside only

MORE TRICKY ONES

427 What surface is ice-hockey played on?
a)Hardened porridge b)Water c)Ice d)Snow

428 If you travelled north from Northampton 3 miles on Thursday, stopped on Friday and travelled north one mile on Saturday, how far from Northampton would you be?
a)4 days b)Tuesday c)4 miles

429 What natural fibre comes from a silkworm?
a)Wool b)Glue c)Silk d)Nylon

430 If you look in a mirror, on which side of your body is your left shoulder?
a)Right b)Left

431 Who painted Van Gogh's self-portrait?
a)Van Gogh b)Van Dyck c)Vanburgh d)Van load

432 What is the brightest star in our sky?
a)The sun b)Betelgeuse c)Sunday

433 On an Ordnance Survey map, what does the symbol for a windpump look like?
a)Church with a steeple b)A square with a corkscrew handle c)Level Crossing d)A windpump

434 What does a downhill racer wear on his feet?
a)Woolly slippers b)Ice skates c)Skis

435 Where is the famous rock called the Old Man of Hoy?
a)Hoy b)Cornwall c)Oswestry d)Off the north coast of Italy

436 What is the book *Treasure Island* about?
a)Three bears b)Princess Diana c)A treasure island

437 There are twice as many coins lying on a table heads up as tails up. If you turn one coin over there are now twice as many coins tail up than heads. How many coins are there?
a)2 b)3 c)6 d)5

438 What is in Autumn, Winter and Spring but not in Summer?
a)Conifer tree's leaves b)5 c)Cricket d)N

439 Can you compile a sentence which has the word HAD occurring consecutively eleven times, and makes perfect sense?
a)Yes b)No

440 If your answer was yes to question 439, do it.

441 Which is the odd square out?

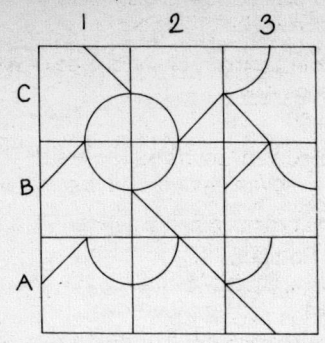

a)B3 b)C3 c)B1 d)A2

442 How many times is the word SET missing from this sentence: 'I played a of tennis against the Dor champion. He was on winning, but I about the task with a large racket and a of old balls. He tled on a draw.
a)4 b)5 c)6 d)7

443 What are the average number of pips in a seedless grape?
a)0 b)1 c)2.3487

ANSWERS

1. b) 3. Barbara has 1 marble, John has 2 marbles, Alan has 6. Total = 9. If each must have 3 (i.e. 9/3) then Alan gives away 3, 2 to Barbara, 1 to John.
2. b) No
3. d) Eve and Sue. Sue is in 'tisSUE factory' and Eve is in 'UnilEVEr'.
4. By telephone.
5. All at Sea. Finishing order is All at Sea, Give us a Kiss, Bright Star, Pottipop.
6. c) Telly people. Substitute 'sm' for 't'.
7. a) 8901. 1861 is 1981 upside-down.
8. c) Can. The story should read: 'A couple of scantily dressed cancan dancers from Cannes, canoed down a canyon in Canada, and saw a toucan eating a potato. If a toucan can do it, can you?'
9. a) Two. **Nine** numbers are to be se**en in** this sen**ten**ce, but someh**ow three** of them are writ**ten o**ut backwards. Which **one** of these backwards numbers i**s even**?'
10. With a long straw.
11. a) College boys oil laboratory doors. The dogs in the other phrases were: b) poodle c) corgi d) pug
12. b) 6. Consider the three containers to start:

	5 litre	3 litre	Other
At the start	5	3	0
After 1st pouring	5	0	3
After 2nd pouring	2	3	3
After 3rd pouring	2	0	6
After 4th pouring	0	2	6
After 5th pouring	5	2	1
After 6th pouring	4	3	1

You end with 4 litres in the 5-litre bucket

13. a) 10
14. a) September. The sequence is in 5-month intervals.
15. b) Saturday. Same number of letters as Thursday.
16. d) Logdog: 'g' substituted for 'n'.
17. The tiger was dead.
18. a) Yes. Two goats at opposite corners of the square can graze only 3½ metres towards the centre which is 3.535 metres from the corner. Therefore a small area in the middle is out of range of all four goats.
19. d)

20 d)Growhat. Growhat = Warthog: the others are a)Kangaroo b)Wallaby c)Wombat.
21 a)Yes – with one of the 10p coins.
22 d)3. If we had 7 sweets then the division of those sweets would be as follows:
    YOU,ME,YOU,ME,YOU,YOU,YOU, i.e. YOU have 5. I have 2. This is of course the same for all odd numbers.
23 b)No chance. There are only two pebbles left.
24 a)Louis. All have three vowels.
25 c)East.
26 b)5
27 a)Spurs. Spurs 6, QPR 5.
28 a)1/3
29 b)
30 b)4
31 b)Right
32 c)Tuffet. Little *Jack* Horner sat in a *corner*, Little Miss Muffet sat on a *tuffet*.
33 d)18. You have 9 pints of milk and tea combined.
34 b)Georg and Laszlo Biró.
35 d)The inside of your eyelids.

QUICKIES

36 c)Singers
37 c)Siam
38 d)David
39 c)The top
40 c)Hazelnuts
41 c)Downstream
42 c)Things far away
43 a)Mayor
44 d)Rose
45 d)Hands

---

46 b)16. From the nursery rhyme 'Half a pound of tuppenny rice, half a pound of treacle . . .'
47 b)Counter-clockwise
48 a)Left.
49 The dovetail joint is drawn on the wrong edge: i.e. piece B does not reach face A.
50 c)The worms reproduce.
51 b)4
52 d)Lay them down flat.
53 c)Horse chestnut.

54 a) Water – the letters are H to O = H$_2$O is the chemical symbol for water.
55 d) Nothing – lines of longitude meet at the poles.
56 b) Knees.
57 d) Weed-killer. After the letters 'S' and 'T' have been reinstated, the letter reads: 'This settlement is surrounded by thistles, please send some killer.'
58 d) Subcontinental. On two counts – facetious and abstemious have all five vowels in alphabetical order, unoriental and subcontinental have all five vowels in reverse alphabetical order. Also the pairs of words have the same endings.
59 d) Q. These are the only letters in the alphabet that enclose space. Q is the next in alphabetical order, R is the last.

OBSERVATION ONE ... THE FAMILY

60 b) 1
61 c) 5
62 c) A dummy.
63 a) Cross.
64 a) 9
65 c) Tom.
66 c) Factory.
67 a) 1
68 c) Horizon line missing.
69 d) Therese.

---

70 c) 1
71 d) You can't tell.
72 d) You can't tell.
73 b) It wouldn't exist if it was torn up.
74 You, the reader.
75 d)
76 c) 9 hours 50 minutes. The letters substituted are B = M, Z = N, T = R, F = T, M = W. The message reads: 'Meet me at ten to ten a.m. tomorrow.'
77 d) Matchbox.
78 c) eslaf si tnemetats dnoces eht. The second statement is true so statement c), 'The second statement is false', is itself false.
79 a) 14. Two children, 4 grandchildren and 8 great-grandchildren = 14.

80 d) 201. Each number is doubled and reversed, i.e. 51 × 2 = 102 reverse = 201.
81 d) A stone.
82 d) After Christ was born.
83 d) They won't. The area of one tile is 5 × 10 = 50cm². This will not go exactly into the total area of the space which is 15 × 15 = 225cm².
84 c) Human flea.
85 b) Black.
86 c) TO. The notice should have read: 'A TOWEL WAS STOLEN FROM THE TOILET TONIGHT. WOULD THE SIMPLETON WHO TOOK IT, PLEASE RETURN IT TO MR TOLLY IN THE STORES TOMORROW.'
87 d) Electricity.
88 b) V. The sequence represents the kings and queens of England in reverse order, i.e.: E 2 = Elizabeth 2, G 6 = George 6, G 5 = George 5, E 7 = Edward 7, V = Victoria.
89 c) Over 90 million miles. We can all see the sun and the stars.
90 c) Penguin.
91 C
92 c) When Queen Elizabeth II became queen.
93 c) q
94 c) It depends where you are.
95 a) Bristol. Travelling east from London, Bristol would be the last place one would get to.
96 c) Silk – a natural fibre produced by silkworms.
97 c) They grow under the ground.

OBSERVATION TWO ... THE SEASIDE

98 c) Rock.
99 d) 'Sh!'
100 a) Book.
101 c) 3.
102 c) Cup.
103 d) A shark.
104 a) Left.
105 a) Sunglasses.
106 b) Right.
107 b) 2 dots.

108 b) No.

109 b)Bulgaria. The letters AGIRL are in buLGARIa.
110 c)None. For instance between 12.02 and 1.02 or between 1.07 and 2.07 etc.
111 d)Nails.
112 Jimmy cannot be an orphan if he died before his mother.
113 b)Not Out.
114 d)All the figures have 12 edges except d), which has ten.

MORE QUICKIES

115 a)Tyne.
116 d)Nothing. The islands are uninhabited.
117 a)Up.
118 b)Hardy.
119 c)Igloo.
120 c)Pluto.
121 c)In a dictionary.
122 a)Moths.
123 a)S.
124 b)Queen Victoria.

125 b)Right.
126 d)
127 a)Yes – 4 wins and a draw.
128 b)T.
129 c)Triangle.
130 c)Woolworths. The initial letters of each word in the message spell out Woolworths.
131 a)4.
132 c)The same amount.
133 c)SDRAWKCAB.
134 d)LBERRAD.
135 c)SOFT. The others are anagrams of each other.
136 d)Missing. What word is 'missing' from this sentence?
137 c)Viola.
138 c)5.

OBSERVATION THREE ... THE STREET

139 a)Left.
140 a)Undertaker's.
141 c)6.
142 c)Dorx.
143 c)V.

144 c)Lampshade.
145 c)Parking meter.
146 a)8.
147 c)Right.
148 c)37.

149 a)3.
150 b)11. Letters in 'the alphabet'.
151 a)10.
152 c)Left elbow.
153 b)Chip.
154 c)6. Splitting the 8 as drawn in half gives you 3. 3 × 2 = 6.
155 c)10 metres.
156 d)It would say 'España', not Spain.
157 No chance, as it would be midnight.
158 b)Tails.
159 c)My son.
160 a)Blackberry. The names and the foods have the same number of double letters and recurring letters.
161 c)Watch.
162 b)20 seconds. It doesn't matter how many ants there are.
163 Denmark. CamDEN MARKet.
164 d)0.
165 a)Pat.
166 b)Monday.
167 There are two 'of's.
168 b)Wall. Humpty Dumpty sat on a wall.
169 a)9.

MORE QUICKIES

170 a)28 February.
171 b)5.
172 c)lpha.
173 a)5 inches. In the other two cases the brick would have been 0 inch or − 1 inch thick.
174 b)Churchill.
175 a)Heads.
176 c)12.
177 d)Mum.
178 b)No.
179 c)L'amour.

180 a)8.
181 c)Ashtray.
182 c)
183 c)3 lines at neck, 5 circles.
184 Line missing at bottom.
185 a)6.
186 d)
187 c)
188 c)0. The first entry of '0' is on the right of the volume as we look at it, the last entry of 'Z' is on the left, therefore '0' and 'Z' must lie next to each other with just the thicknesses of the volumes between them.
189 Peter was a bird.
190 b)Yes. Take a pencil or any other thin long object and 'push the orange through the matchbox lid' with it.
191 d)He mostly pronounces d's as g's. He pronounces the d's in found and and.
192 c)20.
193 d)19. I start with 13 candles, which leaves me enough wax for 4⅓ candles. I burn down the new 4 which leaves me enough for 1⅓ candles. I burn the whole candle which leaves me enough for ⅓ of a candle. The three ⅓s left over each time make another candle, the nineteenth.

OBSERVATION FOUR ... THE ART GALLERY

194 a)XXIVB.
195 a)Umbrella.
196 a)No Entry.
197 a)Left.
198 a)4.
199 c)WAY OUT.
200 c)Table.
201 d)Canneloni's.
202 a)Chewing Gum.
203 b)Lamp.

---

204 d)They end in 'e'.
205 b)The sides of the figures increase by one, the numbers inside increase by two.
206 c)Hen. The letters H E N are in each of the place names.
207 c)SWON.
208 b)O 12 times.

209 b)His widow's cousin. The man would be dead to have a widow.
210 c)Both at the same time. Before BBC2 was introduced there was simply BBC Television and ITV. When the third channel came, the titles BBC1 and BBC2 were assigned to the two channels.
211 b)
212 a)9.
213 a)A cicada, an insect that looks like a cigar.
214 a)Clockwise.
215 d)All the same.
216 a)0 – it's the peahen that lays the eggs.
217 b)Knitting needles. The larger they are the smaller the number.

QUICKIES AGAIN

218 c)50.
219 b)It's the colour of their hair.
220 c)uoy.
221 a)Charles Macintosh.
222 a)1. Pod.
223 c)He isn't older.
224 b)Peahen.
225 c)Cheddar.
226 b) and c). The cuckoo sings 'cuckoo' at the beginning of the season which gradually deteriorates to 'gowk' at the end, before it flies back to Africa. In Scotland the name for a cuckoo is a gowk, and Gowk's Day is 1 April, All Fools' Day.
227 c)Nile.

---

228 a)
229 a)100.
230 c)6. Number 6 is opposite both numbers 9 and 11.
231 c)He split a 'No Smoking' notice in two.
232 b)6. Six coins of equal diameter will exactly fit round a similar coin's edge.
233 c)ROnnie BArker.
234 d)Yob. The others make: a)Amy or May b)Kay c)Ivy.
235 b)2. One boy has eaten 1½ cakes, the other has eaten ½ a cake, i.e. three times more.
236 d)Tolpuddle. Tolpuddle starts with the last three letters of Bristol.
237 Both cars were on a car transporter.

238 d) Feet.
239 a) Missing half a circle on the vase.
240 a) 6. The numbers are in alphabetical order: Eight, Five, Four, Nine, One, Seven, Six.
241 b) 10.
242 He touched him, for Tom was in the boat with Dan.
243 c) A cloudy sky at night.
244 a) Yes.
245 b) 3 – if the five girls all sit together.
246 c) 7 – 3 runs run and 4 in overthrows.
247 b) From the Duke of Wellington.
248 d) Cubic.

OBSERVATION FIVE ... THE COUNTRY

249 a) Milk churn.
250 b) 8.
251 b) 3.
252 a) Left.
253 a) 2.
254 a) Yes – driving the tractor.
255 b) Snow.
256 c) Centre.
257 a) Nearer.
258 b) Deciduous.

---

259 Clive Doig.
260 c) They're dead.
261 c) Blue.
262 a) Yes – bend your knees!
263 c) 1. Ellen starts with the fifth letter of the alphabet, David with the fourth, Josephine with the tenth and Alan the first.
264 a)
265 a) SISAO.

MORE QUICKIES

266 c) Raspberries.
267 c) Two.
268 c) General Franco.
269 a) Round.
270 b) She did.
271 d) Friday.
272 b) Your mouth.
273 b) Bow.

274 c)Elephant.
275 a)Two pounds of feathers.

OBSERVATION SIX ... THE PLANT-POT

276 a)Circles.
277 b)3.
278 b)Ruler.
279 c)A horse.
280 b)2.
281 a)Tray.
282 a)Toothbrush.
283 c)30.
284 b)Lower than it is long.
285 a)Zigzags.

---

286 His horse was called Friday.
287 a)Red, Black and Blue.
288 b)Yes – if it goes over a pulley above him.
289 Jump.
290 d)Telephone dials.
291 c)Devonport. The letters D O G are in each of the answers.
292 a)
293 d)The figures are the numbers 1 to 7 with their vertical reflections to the left. 8 is the next in sequence.
294 d)÷.
295 d)Rod.
296 It was daylight.
297 c)FEET – comes in between FEAT and FRET.
298 d)344. The first pair have 6 after 1 month = 8 rabbits. If each of the baby rabbits has 6 babies then after 7 months another 42 babies are born = 50 rabbits. Given the first pair have 6 babies and each of the other 48 rabbits have six each then after 13 months a further 294 rabbits are born. Grand total = 50 + 294 = 344.
299 c)Rugby. RU(G = half a gee-gee!)BY.
300 a)20: 44 − 24 = 20.
301 d)NV. The letters all sound like names when read out: a)Katie b)Ellen c)Elsie, except d)Envy.
302 c)5. Three 5cm blocks under each of the long legs and two 3cm blocks under the short one.
303 a)4.
304 a)4 inches.

305 Rosemary was a goldfish and was knocked out of her fish bowl by clumsy Fred.
306 a)
307 a)J. December, November, October, September, August, July, June.
308 a)Triangles. 13 – squares 8.
309 a)The motorist wasn't in his car.
310 c)1.
311 b)8.
312 a)Shorter.
313 b)Grandmother.

OBSERVATION SEVEN ... THE BUS

314 c)8.
315 a)Yes.
316 c)97B.
317 b)Tennis racket.
318 a)11.
319 c)Longi Park.
320 d)On a country road.
321 a)Barking dog.
322 a)1.
323 b)Continuous dotted line.

324 b)No.
325 c)4.50.
326 b)4 – number of letters.
327 a)1 hour. To climb 3 metres of the wall in one hour, the snail counters the gravitational force and slipperiness of 2 metres per hour which pulls it down when it stops, therefore its normal rate of travel would be 5 metres an hour. When it is coming down, it has the 2 metres per hour slipperiness and gravitational force to add to its 5 metres per hour, i.e. 7 metres per hour.
328 a)FIG 22. CAT = 24 DECK = 23 MOP = 44.
329 Three blind mice, three blind mice.
330 Little Jack Horner sat in a corner.

MORE TRICKY QUICKIES

331 c)Every month.
332 b)1.
333 d)Walrus.
334 a)North Pole.

335 d) A duck-bill. Another mammal, an echidna, also lays eggs.
336 c) Johann Strauss.
337 a) Nothing.
338 c) The Arctic.
339 d) Pussy willow.
340 d) Eskimo.

---

341 A
342 d) 16.
343 b) They rhyme.
344 e) Pour the contents into glass b).
345 d) For. A force of forty peasants came forth and foraged for a fortnight in the peaceful forests of Fort William.
346 d) R – REAM TRAM TERM TEAR.
347 c) Same shape capitals as small.
348 c)
349 c) Fire of London 1666.
350 b) d.
351 b) West.
352 a) 5.
353 c) Car salesman: CAReful CARl CARter.
354 d)

OBSERVATION EIGHT... THE BOOKSHELF

355 a) The one on the left.
356 c) The one on the left. Peoples of the World, plus maps.
357 d) 8.
358 a) 3 1 2.
359 c) French.
360 b) 2. The Bible and Love Poems.
361 b) The dictionary.
362 b) 6.
363 b) Right.
364 a) 2.

---

365 b) Margaret.
366 b) RANT.
367 c) Half a dozen. Half a dozen baker's dozens = 6 × 13 = 78. Half a dozen dozens = 6 × 12 = 72.
368 c) L.
369 a) Win. Puts a nought in bottom left corner. Crosses cannot stop either of two winning rows.
370 c) 1. A £1 coin.

371 c)1. Only I was going to St Ives.
372 a)3. They each took 3. There were 12 to start, ¼ of 12 = 3, ⅓ of 9 = 3, ½ of 6 = 3.
373 a)5.
374 b)Jack of Clubs.
375 c)1.
376 a)1.
377 b)S. Days of the week, S for Saturday.
378 d)Air.
379 a)0.
380 b)Hannah – they all begin and end with the same letter.
381 c)3. One cut vertically in half, the second vertically in half again, and the third horizontally in half again.
382 a)Back of your ear.
383 c)Dragonfly.
384 b)Right.
385 b)B2.

TRICKY QUICKIES

386 c)Monday.
387 a)Once a year.
388 b)Battle.
389 c)My son's father: i.e. me!
390 b)A nightingale.
391 d)Roses.
392 a)None.
393 a)11. All the months have 30 days except for February.
394 c)Over 12 miles. If he jumped out of an aeroplane that was 12 miles up in the air.
395 d)Danish.

---

396 b)No.
397 c)Ponder. The other words have three consecutive letters of the alphabet in them in alphabetical order. PON is backward order.
398 b)11.
399 h)
400 a)Lose a day.
401 c)Snowdonia.
402 a)31.
403 a)1.
404 b)Pat is a girl.
405 c)Czechoslovakia – it has OSLO at its centre.
406 Blue.

407 d)Taunton: Aunt in ton.
408 c)Nobody.
409 c)Peter. DrainpiPE TERrace.

OBSERVATION NINE ... TINS

410 d)0.
411 b)3.
412 a)Anchovies.
413 c)0.
414 a)Baked Beans.
415 b)Peaches.
416 d)12.
417 b)Tomato Soup.
418 c)Salt-cellar.
419 c)Tuna.

420 The letter F.
421 b)5 litres. Hold one bucket above the other.
422 a)A semicircle.
423 a)Yes. If he said he was not at the scene of the crime and he was lying, then he was there.
424 a)Left.
425 d)River.
426 a)Opposite side to the hinges.

MORE TRICKY ONES

427 c)Ice.
428 c)4 miles.
429 c)Silk.
430 b)Left.
431 a)Van Gogh.
432 a)The sun. It of course is a star.
433 d)A windpump.
434 c)Skis.
435 a)Hoy.
436 c)A treasure island.

437 b)3.
438 d)N.
439 a)Yes – although you might not have been able to do it, it can be done!
440 In an examination, Smith, where Jones had had 'had had', had had 'had', 'had had' had had the examiner's approval.
441 d)A2.

442 c)6. I played a SET of tennis against the DorSET champion. He was SET on winning, but I SET about the task with a large racket and a SET of old balls. He SETtled on a draw.

443 a)0.

Acknowledgements

This 'Beat the Teacher' book is based on the first series transmitted on BBC TV in 1984. The author would like to thank the producer, Ian Oliver, the question-master, Howard Stableford, and especially the schools, without whom there could have been no programmes. Those taking part were: Bedford's Park School, Romford; Brickhill Middle School, Bedford; Fortismere School, London; Impington Village College, Cambridgeshire; King David High School, Liverpool; Monk's Walk School, Welwyn Garden City; St. Bernadette's R.C. School, Bristol and Weald School, Billinghurst, W. Sussex.